"In his previous book, *The Dark Side of Leadership*, Sam Rima puts us in his debt by showing us obstacles that hinder our leadership and by giving us reliable guidance in how to overcome those challenges. In this new book, *Leading from the Inside Out*, Rima takes us to the inner foundations essential for enduring leadership that is able both to withstand attacks from without and to maintain the integrity and equilibrium of the person within."

—Dr. George K. Brushaber, president, Bethel College & Seminary

"Sam Rima has written a vital book for our time! It is a must read for every person who seeks to influence others. I know I was strengthened personally by reading it!"

—Pam Farrel, author and president of Masterful Living

"This is not a book to merely read but a book to do. Grab your journal and your creative thinking to gain some true self insights as you work your way through *Leading from the Inside Out*. Sam Rima's self revelation and discipline sets a strong model for other leaders in this book."

—Dr. Chuck Hiatt, president, North American Baptist Seminary

"In this day of interactive media, Dr. Samuel Rima has produced an important contribution on the subject of leadership. *Leading from the Inside Out* spells out not only important principles but also makes it easy to interact with those principles. I especially appreciate the emphasis on character as there seems to be continually increasing disengagement between character and leadership. This book is well worth reading for those in leadership which, in my opinion, would include all as everyone exerts some level of leadership."

—Dr. Clyde Cook, president, Biola University

"Anyone who is concerned about personal leadership will be challenged and richly blessed by this wise, insightful book. Sam Rima shares deeply out of his rich experiences—including his struggles—as a pastor. And he has obviously read widely and been mentored by leaders whom he trusts. The specific personal exercises at the end of each section are very helpful. All kinds of church leaders—actual and potential—need to read this book and take it to heart."

—Dr. Roger L. Fredrikson, former president, American Baptist Churches

"Sam Rima has stepped into the gap and addressed the most important leadership issue of our day-the discipline of self-leadership. Many have written on the need for character and integrity in leadership, but few have provided a clear path for personal development that is genuinely helpful. Dr. Rima's book, *Leading from the Inside Out*, provides that path in a way that is insightful, practical, and wise."

—DR. JERRY SHEVELAND, VICE PRESIDENT OF GLOBAL CHURCH ENRICHMENT, BAPTIST GENERAL CONFERENCE

"Each day we're a day closer to becoming the persons and leaders we'll ultimately be. That can be a frightening prospect—unless we're intentionally mastering the art of self-leadership now. The decisions and actions Sam Rima advocates in his newest book provide a fundamental structure for leaders to build personal integrity for the long haul as they serve God and His people."

—PAMELA HEIM, DIRECTOR, BAPTIST GENERAL CONFERENCE WOMEN'S MINISTRIES

"In today's economically-driven society, Sam Rima offers readers an opportunity to refocus our eyes, ears, and heart on who we are in Christ. Simply put, this book compels the reader to base his/her leadership style on a biblical frame of reference."

—DR. MARK BENEDETTO, PRESIDENT, UNIVERSITY OF SIOUX FALLS

"Dr. Rima's book on self-leadership is insightful, thorough, and relevant to everyone serving in positions of leadership. He clearly shows the strong relationship beween personal and occupational leadership and its impact on success as a leader. Dr. Rima is a gifted writer who has the ability to state his position clearly and persuasively. This book should be required reading for individuals who serve in leadership roles regardless of whether they work in a secular or non-secular organization."

—DR. TOM McCLUNG, INTERIM DEAN, COLLEGE OF INFORMATION SCIENCES AND TECHNOLOGY, UNIVERSITY OF NEBRASKA, OMAHA

"One of the results of living in a postmodern age is people who struggle with managing their own lives. Both within and without the church, it is clear that a large number of people need to get back to the basics of learning how to balance their physical, emotional, intellectual, and spiritual selves. *Leading from the Inside Out* provides a practical and biblical hands-on resource for assisting all of us to lead our own lives, and those of others, for the glory of God."

—DR. GARY L. McINTOSH, TALBOT SCHOOL OF THEOLOGY, BIOLA UNIVERSITY

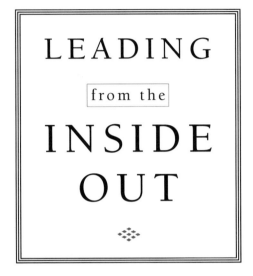

LEADING
from the
INSIDE
OUT

Also by Samuel D. Rima

Overcoming the Dark Side of Leadership (with Gary L. McIntosh)

LEADING

from the

INSIDE

OUT

❖

THE ART OF
SELF-LEADERSHIP

SAMUEL D. RIMA

Baker Books

A Division of Baker Book House Co
Grand Rapids, Michigan 49516

Published by Baker Books
a division of Baker Book House Company
P.O. Box 6287, Grand Rapids, MI 49516-6287

Second printing, January 2002

Printed in the United States of America

Library of Congress Cataloging-in-Publication Data is on file at the Library of Congress, Washington, D.C.

ISBN 0-8010-9104-7

Unless otherwise indicated, Scripture quotations are taken from the *Holy Bible,* New Living Translation, copyright © 1996. Used by permission of Tyndale House Publishers, Inc., Wheaton, IL 60189. All rights reserved.

Scripture quotations marked NASB are taken from the NEW AMERICAN STANDARD BIBLE®. Copyright © The Lockman Foundation 1960, 1962, 1963, 1968, 1971, 1973, 1975, 1977, 1995. Used by permission.

For current information about all releases from Baker Book House, visit our web site:
http://www.bakerbooks.com

This book is dedicated to the inaugural class of the Leadership Central program:

Neil Downey
Barry Milbauer
Ann Tschetter
Randy Maass
Kay Hodges
Landon Ludens
Jane Fahlberg
Jenny Downey
Jeff Reynolds
Loren Mendel
Jim Subert
Brad Paulson
John Lang

As we spent time learning to lead our lives, I have come to love each of you more than I can say.

And to . . .
The future leaders I live with every day:

Jill
Seth
Hillary
Sammy

I pray that you will learn to lead and live your life well so that others will want to follow.

Contents

Acknowledgments

I want to express my thanks and appreciation to my wife, Sue. She is truly my inspiration and once again provided the support and encouragement for me to complete this book. She willingly sacrificed spending many of my days off with me so that I could write, joining me instead for a cup of coffee at my makeshift office at our local Barnes and Noble. On each of those occasions she brought with her the encouragement I needed to complete the remainder of that day's work. Sue, this book is yours as much as it is mine. I love you!

Also I want to express my deepest thanks and gratitude to Kay Hodges for her tireless work on this manuscript during time that would have otherwise been her own. Very simply, the final stages of this book would have been intolerably difficult to complete without her able assistance. This book bears her insightful and professional touch. Kay wrote the study questions for chapter 6 and provided other helpful suggestions throughout the process. She never failed to smile when I entered her office with yet another version or wild idea for a chapter already completed. I am grateful for her help but, more important, I am grateful for her friendship and the privilege of serving together on the same ministry team.

I am also grateful to the fellows, members, and sponsors of the Leadership Central Foundation, who provided the support necessary to launch this leadership program and test this material in the "real world." I pray that we will see our efforts multiplied countless times as God graciously uses the program to develop leaders for his kingdom.

As always, I am indebted to the work of my editor, Paul Engle. His interest in this project and e-mail notes of encouragement have helped me to believe that God can use me as a writer. Also this book that you now hold has been made eminently more readable by the skillful editing of Mary Suggs. Thanks for your work, Mary! Additionally, I want to thank Sara Metzger, the interview coordinator at Baker, for the work I know she will do to help get the word out about this book. Sara, your work on behalf of *Overcoming the Dark Side of Leadership* is greatly appreciated!

And to the staff team at Central Baptist Church I am eternally grateful. I love you all and count it a blessing to go to work each day. What a fantastic team! You are All Stars!

INTRODUCTION

When Vice President Al Gore made the official announcement, declaring himself a candidate for president of the United States in the year 2000, he spoke from the steps of the Smith County Courthouse in his hometown of Carthage, Tennessee. During that speech, he made one comment in particular that grabbed my attention. He spoke about the serious deficits that were plaguing our culture—a decency deficit, a time deficit, a moral deficit, and a deficit in personal and cultural values. Then, with more passion than I can ever remember hearing from him, the vice president said that the only way our cultural deficits could be cured was by people once again taking seriously the need for self-mastery. The vice president seemed to say that our culture would only be able to recover from its deplorable condition if Americans recaptured the values that used to be commonly held in our country. Further, he asserted that such a recovery would only be possible when individuals began taking seriously their need to master their own personal life and live with stronger personal values and morals, which would guide their public behavior.

AN OLD MESSAGE WITH NEW URGENCY

The vice president's message about the need for renewed self-mastery was nothing new, but there seemed to be a new sense of urgency for implementing and living out this age-old principle.

In his venerable classic, *Lectures to My Students,* addressed to those poised to enter the ranks of spiritual leadership, Charles Haddon Spurgeon began his advice by writing:

> We are, in a certain sense, our own tools, and therefore must keep ourselves in order. If I want to preach the gospel, I can only use my own voice; therefore I must train my vocal powers. I can only think with my own brain, and feel with my own heart, and therefore I must educate my intellectual and emotional faculties. I can only weep and agonise for souls in my own renewed nature, therefore must I watchfully maintain the tenderness which was in Christ Jesus. It will be in vain for me to stock my library, or organise societies, or project schemes, if I neglect the culture of myself; for books, and agencies, and systems, are only remotely the instruments of my holy calling; my own spirit, soul, and body, are my nearest machinery for sacred service; my spiritual faculties, and my inner life, are my battle axe and weapons of war.

Spurgeon goes on to say,

> For the herald of the gospel to be spiritually out of order in his own proper person is, both to himself and to his work, a most serious calamity; and yet, my brethren, how easily is such an evil produced, and with what watchfulness must it be guarded against! . . . a man in all other respects fitted to be useful may by some small defect be exceedingly hindered, or even rendered utterly useless.[1]

Spurgeon rightly recognized that the ultimate success of a leader will be determined by how well he or she masters the inner life. He saw all other skills, talents, and gifts only as effective as the foundation on which they are built—that foundation being the leader's inner life.

In recent years it seems that this principle of self-mastery, or what I have labeled self-leadership, as the foundation for effective leadership has been discarded in favor of a more pragmatic approach. Today's leaders seem to be judged more on what they are able to produce than on who they are as people. The general consensus during recent years seems to have been that it doesn't matter what a leader is like in private as long as he or she can fulfill the public role and produce the prosperity that followers have come to expect as our American birthright. But our willingness to exchange character-driven leadership for production-driven leadership has, I would contend, brought our culture and nation to the brink of implosion. If we are not successful at restoring self-leadership as the primary foundation for leadership, we are likely to witness a further crumbling of our presently fragile culture.

ONLY AS STRONG AS OUR FOUNDATION

The story is told of a new firehouse that was built in Pennsylvania sometime during the last century. It was built using some of the most revolutionary architectural principles of the time and the newest building materials available. It was a beautiful new building that soon became the talk of the region, drawing people from all over the county who came to marvel at this miracle of modern science and technology.

Surprisingly, after only a few months of use, the shiny new building began to show signs of trouble. First, cracks began to appear between the ceiling and the top of the doorjambs. Not too much later, certain areas of the floor started to buckle to the extent that they were declared unsafe for people to walk on. Then the doors and windows would not close or open. Finally, the roof began to buckle to the point that shingles were beginning to fall off.

Ultimately the marvelous new building had to be condemned by the city authorities. And before long the entire structure almost seemed to implode as it fiercely crumpled to the ground, leaving nothing but a heap of rubble where the once proud testament to modern technology had stood.

Because of the way this new building deteriorated so quickly, the authorities investigated the possible causes of the firehouse's premature demise. After a lengthy study, it was determined that the cause of the problem was a moderately sized fissure in the foundation that went unnoticed during the initial inspections. Compounding the danger created by the weakness in the foun-

15

dation was the fact that an underground river deep beneath the surface was slowly eroding the ground directly below the fractured foundation. Though the building looked great at ground level, beneath the surface there lurked some flaws in the foundation that eventually caused the entire structure to crumble.

FLAWS IN OUR LEADERSHIP FOUNDATION

Recently we have seen a similar story played out within the ranks of leadership across our nation and, indeed, throughout the entire world. We had become enamored with the popular leaders of national and international renown, whether they exercised their leadership in the realm of the church, government, or private enterprise. People aspiring to positions of leadership flocked to gawk at those leaders and learn the latest in leadership technology. From all outward appearances the leaders looked like models of strength, composure, and self-control. However, it wasn't long before the nation began to notice some curious signs that something might be wrong in the lives and practice of many of these marquee heads of church and state.

During the past fifteen to twenty years, we have all watched in astonishment as one effective leader after another has crashed and burned, resulting in public humiliation for the leader, their families, as well as the organizations to which they gave leadership.

After much inquiry and investigation into the causes of these public leadership failures, it has been discovered that the primary culprit in virtually every case has been a flaw in the failed leader's personal foundation. Though the leader may have been gifted, intelligent, and apparently extremely effective, there were fissures in the foundation that had either escaped notice or had been purposely ignored.

Unfortunately, however, just as with the marvelous new firehouse, the flaws in the foundations of these leaders began to become more and more noticeable. But because the problem was deep beneath the surface, most of these leaders crashed and burned before the appropriate repairs could be made.

We have all witnessed a president, esteemed congressional leaders, top-level business executives, nationally known ministers and denominational officials, as well as countless other prominent leaders suffer humiliating failures as a result of serious flaws in their personal foundation. Though without exception these leaders had risen to lofty levels of leadership based on their effective application of essential leadership skills and use of the most recent leadership technologies, no amount of skill or delivery of success could forestall their eventual failure. When there are serious flaws in a foundation, whether that foundation belongs to a building or a leader, those flaws will always compromise the integrity of what the foundation was intended to support and, if repairs are not made, will eventually result in tragedy.

THE FOUNDATION OF SELF-LEADERSHIP

Leading from the Inside Out was written to assist leaders, as well as aspiring leaders, in doing the all-important foundation work necessary before leadership of integrity can be exercised and maintained.

As in any important construction effort, it is often those issues and elements that are not readily seen that are the most crucial. What is the likelihood of constructing a building that will stand the test of time without quality architectural and engineering work being done well before the first hole for the foundation is ever dug? Ultimately a building will be only as sturdy and resilient as its foundation.

So it is with leadership. Before we can expect to exercise effective leadership that will withstand the hostile elements of our culture, serious preparatory work must be done on those areas of a leader's life that will provide a firm foundation on which an effective leadership career can be built.

The primary assumption of this book is that all effective, enduring leadership must be built on the foundation of effective self-leadership. It is our ability to successfully lead our own life that provides the firm foundation from which we can lead others.

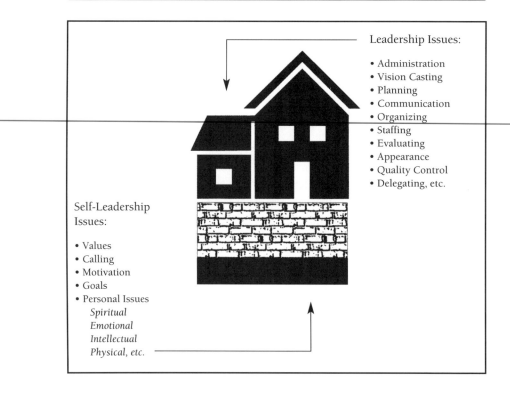

Leadership Issues:

- Administration
- Vision Casting
- Planning
- Communication
- Organizing
- Staffing
- Evaluating
- Appearance
- Quality Control
- Delegating, etc.

Self-Leadership Issues:

- Values
- Calling
- Motivation
- Goals
- Personal Issues
  Spiritual
  Emotional
  Intellectual
  Physical, etc.

The above diagram reflects how effective self-leadership (the foundation) relates to the other aspects of leadership.

BUILDING A FIRM FOUNDATION FROM WHICH TO LEAD

Giving attention to the issues of self-leadership will enable us to build a firm foundation from which we can exercise our leadership. In his classic work *Discipline and Discovery,* Albert Edward Day writes:

We have talked much of salvation by faith, but there has been little realization that all real faith involves discipline. Faith is not a blithe "turning it all over to Jesus." Faith is such confidence in

18

Jesus that it takes seriously his summons, "If any man will come after me, let him deny himself, and take up his cross, and follow me." We have loudly proclaimed our dependence upon *the grace of God, never guessing that the grace of God is given only to those who practice the grace of self-mastery* (emphasis in original).[2]

Day's words reflect the apostle Paul's attitude, as revealed in Scripture, that he was not only an avid adherent of the grace of God but also a fierce advocate of self-discipline. He stated, "I discipline my body like an athlete, training it to do what it should" (1 Cor. 9:27). Paul often used the imagery of a disciplined athlete in his references to how he lived as a leader of Christ's church. Paul took seriously the need to manage his inner life and those foundational issues, such as his personal values and Calling, if he was to be as useful to God as possible. The great apostle lived with the constant awareness that his failure to manage his inner life well could actually result in his own personal stumbling, thus negatively affecting all he had worked so hard to accomplish as an apostle.

Leading from the Inside Out is written with the hope that leaders, who are serious about leading well, leading long, and finishing well, will give serious attention to the issues of self-leadership, which form the only foundation from which they can exercise effective leadership for the glory of God. It is only leaders such as these who can restore public confidence in our institutions and the people who give them leadership.

How to Use This Book

Leading from the Inside Out is divided into three parts. The first part addresses the foundational issues that are necessary for effective self-leadership. You will be challenged to consider the importance of your personal life values and the need to clearly connect with God's Calling for you and to take stock of your current level of motivation to engage in effective self-leadership. Part 1 will also address the importance of developing meaningful life goals toward which you can lead your life.

Part 2 of the book explores the venues in which self-leadership will need to be exercised in your life as a leader. Once you have clarified your values, connected with your Calling, determined your level of motivation, and laid out some worthy life goals, you must actually begin to master the art of self-leadership in the constellation of venues that comprise your life, daily living out your values, Calling, and goals in each arena.

Just as with any organization, there are many forces that will conspire against you in your efforts to realize your values, Calling, and mission. Part 2 gives very practical suggestions for how you can effectively exercise spiritual self-leadership, physical self-leadership, emotional self-leadership, and intellectual self-leadership.

At the end of each chapter 2 through 9, there is a Self-Leadership Workshop that will give you the opportunity to immediately implement the principles you have just read. At the end of part 1 you will be guided through the process of synthesizing what you have done in each of the chapter workshops into a Personal Constitution. This will provide you with a document that you can then use as a guide for decision making and personal direction (in conjunction with Scripture). At the conclusion of part 2 you will bring all of the workshops from chapters 6 through 9 together into a single Self-Leadership Plan that can guide you through the process of systematic, incremental growth in your exercise of self-leadership.

Part 3 contains study guides that can be used to lead group discussions of the material or as the basic framework for presentation curriculum. Though the temptation may be to rush quickly through the reading and begin working through the workshop sections of the book, I strongly encourage you to thoroughly read all the chapters as they will provide the necessary understanding and constructs that will enhance the effectiveness of the workshop in your personal life.

PART 1

FOUNDATIONS
FOR SELF-LEADERSHIP

1

WHY SELF-LEADERSHIP?

In the summer of 1997 the president of the National Baptist Convention, Henry Lyons, was unceremoniously thrust into the national limelight when his wife was arrested for attempting to set fire to a luxury home he owned in south Florida. As the story unfolded, it was learned that this leader's wife was reacting to the recent discovery that her husband had purchased the 700,000-dollar home with his female assistant, whose name was also on the mortgage. As the media pursued the story, additional details came to light that called into question not only the integrity but also the moral standing of this national religious leader. Allegations were made of other extravagant and questionable purchases: a Mercedes Benz automobile, ostensibly for official use, and jewelry worth hundreds of thousands of dollars. Under this developing cloud of controversy, Lyons was brought before a gathering of his denomination for a vote of confidence. Almost unbelievably, this leader received a vote of confidence and remained in his position of leadership, even while a significant segment of the denomination's faithful called for him to step down. His marriage was unquestionably in a state of disarray, his financial practices were at best suspect, and yet he remained in leadership.

THE LOST ART OF SELF-LEADERSHIP

During the decade of the 1990s, in the face of numerous high-profile leadership failures among the ranks of business, political, and even religious leaders, a disturbing but apparently popular philosophy of leadership began to emerge. As more and more leaders were discovered to be leading personal lives characterized by highly questionable behavior, the public has been told that a leader's personal life does not necessarily have an impact on his or her exercise of leadership. The most important issue when selecting leaders is whether they can do the job. Do they have the experience, gifts, and ability to fill the position? That, and that alone, should determine a potential leader's fitness to lead.

When the House Judiciary Committee of the United States Congress voted to pursue a full impeachment inquiry against the president of the United States, Bill Clinton, Americans were forced to think about what qualifies a person to be a leader. The president's reckless, immoral, and self-destructive "private," personal behavior had clouded both terms of his presidency. As a result, our nation experienced a period of unprecedented turmoil and political infighting as pundits and experts filled the public airwaves with pontifications regarding how a leader's personal, private behavior is no one's business and that what they do in private should not in any way be confused with their public exercise of leadership. Thus the debate has been framed: Is a leader's personal life and private behavior in any way germane to his exercise of public leadership?

One side in this raging and, at times, highly emotional debate insists that there is a clear dichotomy and separation between what a leader does in private and what she does in public. The argument goes something like this: A leader's private behavior is immaterial to his exercise of leadership in the public arena. As long as a leader is able to skillfully accomplish the tasks required of the post and can produce positive results, it should not matter to anyone what beliefs that leader privately embraces or what behaviors he or she engages in behind closed doors.

In other words, it seems that the adherents of this position have sold out to pragmatism at the expense of integrity and character. If a leader can produce positive results, who cares about the moral or intellectual underpinnings of his or her life? If a pastor can develop a well-organized sermon and deliver it with panache, then what does it matter that he regularly cheats on his income tax or is a closet racist. If a CEO can produce a healthy bottom line and increase the shareholder's earnings per share, what should it matter that he is a closet alcoholic who enjoys child pornography in the privacy of his own home? As absurd and admittedly ridiculous as these scenarios are, they do represent the logical conclusion of such a position.

This discontinuity between a leader's private life and his public leadership has become rather alarming to those concerned with integrity and character. The argument is based on the faulty premise that a leader's deeply held values and beliefs are not consequential or in any way causative when it comes to his public behavior and the manner in which he exercises his leadership on the public stage. In the past, if this were actually true of a person, if there existed such a breach between beliefs and behavior, that person would be considered psychotic and suffering from some form of psychological integration problem. However, today we are told that such a dichotomy is acceptable and should be respected. The reality is, however, that people who consistently engage in behavior that is contrary to their own values and beliefs are either emotionally or psychologically unhealthy, or both. Such individuals should not be placed in positions of leadership, but should be receiving professional help and supervision. The foundation of all effective, healthy leadership must be the leader's personal character.

This relatively recent view of what qualifies an individual to exercise leadership is indeed a curious development. Are we actually to believe that a legitimate dichotomy can exist between the way a leader conducts her private, personal life and the way she conducts her public leadership? Is it really true that a person's

25

spiritual belief system will have absolutely no influence or bearing on the way he exercises leadership? Can it be believed that a leader who fails to honor personal contracts and pledges should be trusted to honor the contracts and pledges made in her role as a leader? When a person lies to his spouse and children, can he be expected to deal differently with those he leads? If a leader cannot manage her own personal relationships and satisfactorily resolve personal conflicts, is it not blindly optimistic to expect that she can somehow do so in a leadership role?

Though the answers to these questions should be, and at one time were, obvious, they are no longer quite as obvious as one might expect. In fact the reality is that there are leaders in virtually every field who have exercised relatively good leadership in their professional capacity for extended periods of time, while at the same time their personal lives have been in a state of chaos. Eventually, and almost without exception, the time comes when the chaos of the leader's personal life destructively intersects with his or her apparently well-ordered public life, and the result is almost always a scandalous headline or a provocative segment on a TV news magazine. It seems apparent that a person's private life always has a bearing on the exercise of his or her public leadership.

What is the source of this accepted incongruity between a leader's public persona and exercise of leadership and the way that person conducts his personal, private life? Where does this strange notion come from? And how is it possible that a person can be an effective leader in an organizational setting and yet fail miserably in the leadership of her own life?

During the last thirty years, there has been a literal deluge of literature dealing with effective leadership practices and techniques. Countless volumes have been written on the intricacies of influence, vision casting, goal setting, master planning, human resource management, negotiating, administration, and a plethora of other topics pertinent to the exercise of effective organizational leadership. As a result of this emphasis on leadership, there has been a marked increase in the quality and technical effectiveness of the leaders coming out of seminaries and business schools. Paradoxically, during this same period, there seems to have been a noticeable decrease, at least until recently, in the emphasis on the leader's need to develop personal character and to exercise skillful, effective self-leadership.

The response to this shift away from the intentional character development of leaders has been the increase we now witness in public cynicism and disrespect directed toward those in public leadership. Whether it is in the church, business, or politics, people have clearly grown more wary and frustrated with many of our leaders. Gone are the days when a position of leadership garnered immediate and almost unquestionable respect from followers or the general public. To the contrary, today's leaders must invest great effort to prove to those they lead that they are, indeed, credible leaders who are trustworthy. Once established, the continued maintenance of this credibility is a central job for every leader.

The epidemic of public cynicism directed toward leaders is a direct result of the disparity people often perceive between the public and private lives of their leaders. As the media increasingly exposes the personal failure of leaders, it becomes more and more difficult for people to trust any leadership. "If he can't even exercise leadership over his own libido, how can he exercise leadership over the church?" parishioners wonder. Employees and colleagues rightly ask, "If she can't manage her own finances, how can she give leadership to the organization?"

The reality is that the way in which a leader conducts his personal life does, in fact, have a profound impact on his ability to exercise effective public leadership. There is a direct correlation between self-leadership and public leadership. Not until leaders begin to exercise the same quality of leadership over their personal lives that they do in their professional lives will we begin to see the current tide of public cynicism and mistrust toward leaders turn in a more positive direction.

What Is Self-Leadership?

Well, what exactly is self-leadership? What is it that I am promoting when I suggest that leaders need to exercise the same quality of leadership over their own lives that they do in their formal positions of leadership?

Today there are many popular and broadly accepted definitions of leadership as it applies to the leading of organizations and groups of people. All of these definitions make a clear distinction between management and leadership. In times past the terms *management* and *leadership* were often used interchangeably—all people in positions of management were assumed to be leaders. Today that is not the case. Warren Bennis, one of today's most prolific writers on the subject of leadership, makes a clear distinction between leadership and management in his book *On Becoming a Leader*.[1] The manager, according to Bennis, is preoccupied with doing things right. That is, the manager is focused on following procedures and gaining compliance from those she manages. It is a role in which the successful execution of established practices and adherence to standard policies determine the effectiveness of the manager. On the other hand, the leader, Bennis argues, is concerned with doing the right things. Rather than simply executing existing procedures and gaining compliance with accepted practices, the true leader will first question whether or not the accepted procedures are the right thing to do. The true leader is the one who may determine that existing practices are no longer moving the organization in the direction of its vision and mission and create a whole new set of procedures and practices. Rather than being content to transact business within the parameters of the existing paradigm, the leader looks to transform the existing system into something more effective. In essence, according to Bennis, leadership is by its very nature transformational rather than transactional.

Another popular writer and lecturer in the field of leadership is Dr. John Maxwell. To Maxwell, leadership is influence. While Bennis may focus on the end result of a leader's activity (transforming existing paradigms), Maxwell's focus is on the means to that end—the exercise of influence. Effective leaders are those who can influence individuals and organizations in such a compelling way that they are willing to change existing paradigms.

In his classic work, *Leadership,* Pulitzer-prize winning author James MacGregor Burns states that the role of a leader is to mobilize institutional, political, psychological, and other resources to realize mutually beneficial goals.[2]

To summarize, then, effective organizational leaders are able to transform existing paradigms and practices through their use of influence and the mobilization of necessary resources to realize something more beneficial and more effective at achieving their group's or organization's stated mission.

By promoting the concept of self-leadership, I am suggesting that leaders must be vigilant to do the same thing in the leading of their own lives. This is the art of self-leadership. We must constantly be asking whether the existing paradigms in our lives must be transformed. Are the ways we are currently doing things and conducting our lives enabling us to realize our personal mission and purpose? Do we even know what our personal life mission is with the same clarity that we know our organizational mission? If not, why not? Do we consistently exercise influence over our own lives? Can we influence ourselves to make the changes necessary to become more productive and effective human beings and leaders? Do we have the ability to influence ourselves to change the destructive habits and practices that may be keeping us from realizing our full potential? How effective are we at mobilizing the various resources in our own life—physical, intellectual, spiritual, emotional, and financial—to achieve the beneficial goals we have determined will move us in the direction of our life mission? These are the critical issues that must be addressed if we are to master the art of self-leadership.

Effective leaders often do all of these things in their organizational settings, sometimes to the point of obsession, while at the same time they neglect to apply the very same principles to their own lives. The result of this neglect, in many instances, has produced the current climate of cynicism and mistrust that plagues many leaders and the institutions to which they give leadership.

How can it be that a leader is able to create an organization that is the envy of colleagues and competitors alike, yet at the same time preside over a marriage and family that is literally falling apart at the seams? What allows a leader to develop an organization that is healthy and vibrant, while the leader himself is grossly overweight and struggles with his own personal health and fitness?

How can pastors and spiritual leaders give sound financial leadership to their church or nonprofit organization and at the same time experience a personal financial life that is on the verge of collapse? The sad reality is that there are many leaders who have crafted brilliant, inspiring mission statements for their organization, but they cannot clearly articulate an equally inspiring mission statement for their own life.

It is time that leaders, particularly spiritual leaders, begin to master the art of self-leadership to the same degree that they have mastered and practiced the techniques of organizational leadership. If a leader's life does not reflect the same degree of excellence and skill that is manifested in the organization to which she gives leadership, it will eventually result in a dissonance that will erode the trust and respect of those being led. In today's environment, where significant leadership failures are frequent in virtually every arena and there exists a pervasive cynicism and lack of trust directed toward those in leadership, mastering the art of self-leadership has never been more essential to the achievement of effective, holistic leadership.

A Theology of Self-Leadership

What, if anything, does the Bible have to say about self-leadership? Is it biblical or just another self-help philosophy, the focus of which is entirely human? Well, not surprisingly, the Bible has an enormous amount to say about the importance of self-leadership. In the apostle Paul's instructive letters to his youthful protégé, Timothy, Paul speaks often of the need for Timothy to pay close attention to the manner in which he conducts his own life. In fact it is safe to say that Paul focuses more on Timothy's self-leadership than he does on giving specific techniques and tools for the organizational leadership of the church for which Timothy was responsible.

At the very beginning of his first letter to Timothy, Paul strongly urges the young leader to "fight the good fight, keeping faith and a good conscience, which some have rejected and suffered shipwreck" (1 Tim. 1:18–19 NASB). It was important to Paul that Timothy's personal life of faith and practice be consistent with his public life as a leader. Failure to exercise this self-leadership could result in serious failure.

When Paul lists for Timothy the qualifications for potential leaders in the church, his list could not stress the importance of effective self-leadership more clearly. Paul states that the potential leader must be

> above reproach, the husband of one wife, temperate, prudent, respectable, hospitable . . . not addicted to wine or pugnacious, but gentle, uncontentious, free from the love of money. *He must be one who manages his own household well, keeping his children under control with all dignity (but if a man does not know how to manage his own household, how will he take care of the church of God?)*
>
> 1 Timothy 3:2–5 NASB, emphasis mine

In essence, Paul is saying that if a leader cannot effectively lead his own life and household, what business does he have giving leadership to the church or any other organization? It is a principle that seems almost ridiculous in its simplicity! Of course! If a person can't effectively lead his own life and control himself, how should he be expected to provide effective leadership to others? It makes perfect sense. It is absurd and naive to think otherwise. And yet today we are being told that the way a person conducts her personal life has little or nothing to do with her ability to provide leadership on a broader scale.

Paul goes on to instruct Timothy that he should "discipline [himself] for the purpose of godliness" (4:7). Now we know that Paul is not suggesting that Timothy is able to *become* godly through the sheer exercise of personal discipline. Growing in godliness is a work of the Holy Spirit within us. However, it is through the exercise of personal discipline that we are positioned to allow the Holy Spirit to do his sanctifying work more effectively and consistently in us. It is the practice of certain disciplines that, in a manner of speaking, place us in the soil necessary for ongoing spiritual growth and development. Conversely, the failure to exercise these disciplines in our lives will undermine the Spirit's

31

working. Paul goes on to encourage Timothy to live his life in such a way that no one can look down on him and question his leadership (v. 12), but rather he should exercise the discipline necessary to be an example to those he leads. In fact Paul exhorts Timothy: "Take pains with these things; be absorbed in them, so that your progress may be evident to all" (v. 15 NASB). Finally, Paul tells Timothy: "Pay close attention to yourself and to your teaching; persevere in these things" (v. 16 NASB). Paul addresses both the need for faithful, effective self-leadership (pay close attention to yourself), as well as the need for faithful public leadership (and your teaching).

Throughout the Scriptures there are myriad instructions to leaders and potential leaders to exercise effective self-leadership. A case in point would be the tragic story of the Old Testament priest Eli. In 1 Samuel 2 we read the disturbing story of a spiritual leader who failed to exercise self-leadership and suffered severe loss as a result. This aging leader occupied the lofty position of priest but failed to govern his own affairs. In spite of stern warnings regarding his role and responsibility as a leader (see vv. 27–29), he failed in his exercise of leadership at a crucial time in his nation's history. Eli was only too willing to overlook or ignore areas of personal behavior that he felt didn't directly impact the exercise of his formal leadership as priest. However, we see in the sacred text that God places more value on the life of the leader than on his practice of leadership. Ultimately, because of Eli's sloppy personal life, God rather unceremoniously removed him from leadership and brought discipline on his entire family for generations in the future (vv. 31–33).

Additionally, we see throughout the biblical text that when leaders have failed to exercise self-leadership over their emotions and actions, it has almost always bled through their personal lives to negatively impact the organizations and people they led. One obvious example is Moses' failure to exercise self-leadership over his emotions when he impetuously struck the rock rather than speaking to it as God instructed and the serious repercussions of his failure. Then there is Solomon and his lavish lifestyle. His violation of the commands in Deuteronomy 17 and his selfishly taxing the people in excess not only had a negative impact on his son but eventually led to a divided kingdom. We are also aware of David's failure to exercise consistent self-leadership and the devastating effects his failures had on himself and the nation. The examples of Saul, Jonah, Abraham, and others are sprinkled across the pages of Scripture to remind us of the importance of self-leadership in the life of a public leader. At the same time, we have the examples of Esther, Joseph, Daniel, Nehemiah, Paul, and many others whose lives bore the fruit of effective self-leadership.

FAILING TO LEAD YOUR LIFE

In the time it took me to finish writing chapter 1 and get it to the publisher, the Reverend Henry Lyons, president of the National Baptist Convention (NBC), was officially charged with fifty-six counts of fraud, extortion, money laundering, conspiracy, and tax evasion. (He has since been found guilty and is serving nine and one-half years in a Florida prison. Not exactly a great legacy for a leader to leave.) In addition to the shame and embarrassment his reckless exercise of leadership inflicted on him and his family, not to mention the cause of Christ, the National Baptist Convention was thrown into a state of inner turmoil and chaos as members wrangled over what to do about the Reverend Lyons.

As always in these sad cases, there are still a significant number of members within the ranks of the NBC who support their clay-shod leader, in spite of his nefarious behavior. At the same time there is a healthy number who are incensed by their president's behavior and who pushed for his removal and discipline. Such is the price (organizational ineffectiveness) to be paid when leaders fail to take leadership of their own lives. It is a price that many organizations cannot afford to pay and results in their untimely demise. During the waning years of the twentieth century, we as a nation were being forced to determine the price—in a lowered moral standard of leadership, an increase in public cynicism, and international humiliation—that we were willing to pay for President Clinton's failure to exercise effective self-leadership.

Stretching our government and its institutions to the point of internal disruption, the cost was way too high.

MASTERING THE ART OF SELF-LEADERSHIP

The purpose of this book is to encourage and help equip leaders and potential leaders to master the art of self-leadership. Few things are more essential if we are to realize the full potential God has given us as leaders and accomplish all he has called, guided, and gifted us to accomplish through the leadership positions in which he has graciously placed us or prepared for us.

Now, with God's help, it is time to begin so that we might realize our life's full potential as a leader for his glory.

2

ARTICULATING AND EMBRACING YOUR LIFE'S VALUES

As we have seen in the previous chapter, the failure to effectively exercise consistent leadership over one's own life can result in significant failure both for leaders personally and for the organizations they lead. Often high-level leaders are intimately familiar with the core values that guide their organization and, in fact, serve as the primary evangelist of those values within the organization. However, those same leaders who are zealous for their church's or company's values often have no clear idea of what their own personal core values are. In their role as a leader they are value driven, yet in the leading of their own life they often violate the very values they promote professionally.

In July of 1998 it was reported nationally that the director and leader of the government program HEARTS (an acronym for Honesty, Ethics, Accountability, Respect, Trust, and Support) pled guilty to the theft of public funds. In her role as a leader and teacher of honesty, accountability, ethics, and trust, Juddith Ann Gunderson knowingly and intentionally filed false expense reports in an effort to defraud the government of money. Here was a leader, entrusted with the task of instructing and leading others in the development and practice of sound ethics, honesty, and trust, who was practicing the exact opposite in her own life. No doubt she was a hearty proponent of the values she represented in her role as leader of HEARTS, yet somehow those values were not her own deeply held personal values. Amazingly, in spite of the indictment against her and her guilty plea, it was determined that this public leader was still qualified to keep her government position.[1]

CHARACTER COUNTS

Personal character can be defined as the integration of an individual's personal beliefs, values, and morals, which, taken as a whole, reveal the true nature or character of that individual. It is a leader's personal character, then, that determines how he will react to certain situations and determines the priorities that will inform that leader's decisions. A well-integrated person is one for whom there is noticeable continuity between her privately held values and beliefs and her public behavior.

In fact, despite his chronic violation of this principle, even President John F. Kennedy repeatedly proclaimed the connection between sterling character and political greatness. Character, he declared correctly, was a major well-spring of behavior.[2] John Kennedy was not alone in his assessment of the vital nature of personal character (as we defined it above) and performance as a leader. The Greek philosopher and political thinker Aristotle postulated that the only way one can judge the character of another is on the basis of his or her behavior. According to Aristotle, those placed in positions of public leadership should be able to consistently control their baser desires and inclinations out of a genuine desire to promote the public welfare. The best government, to Aristotle's way of thinking, was the government whose leaders publicly acted out their deeply held personal virtues and morality in such a way that they advanced the general tenor of the state.

THE LITMUS OF BEHAVIOR

Though not a popular concept in today's relativistic society where morality and virtue are proclaimed to be ethereal and impossible for one person to define or proscribe for another, the reality is that an individual's behavior is the most accurate indicator of his true character. Ultimately our behavior is simply the acting out of our deeply held values. This in no way suggests that we always like or endorse those things that we value. Quite to the contrary, we may, in fact, be quite disheartened and disgusted with ourselves for the things we value and we will be confronted by our unappealing and destructive values through behaviors that are problematic for us and for those with whom we interact. Because that is often the case, we must honestly and continually assess our values and explore why it is they have come to be values for us. If we are not satisfied with the values we hold, it is up to us to change them.

For example, we may value instant gratification of our material desires. Though intellectually we know that such a value may not be fiscally healthy for us, for whatever reason the instant gratification that immediate purchases provide is still important to us and we allow it to stand. Thus this value will unavoidably drive our behavior in this area of our life. However, after several years of acting out this value in the behavior of compulsive spending and experiencing the financial difficulty that inevitably results, the pain may become so great that we begin to place a higher value on fiscal soundness and financial responsibility than we place on instant gratification. This is the beginning for all lasting behavioral change, showing how our behavior reflects our true values.

When the behavior of public leaders is reckless and self-destructive, causing significant failures, the source of the problem is always the deeply held values of the leader. Whether those values are a need to please others, the personal approval of others, the desire to numb emotional pain, or the need for physical gratification, they will ultimately determine the leader's behavior until they are no longer so greatly valued. In respect to this conflict that all leaders face with values that provide some

37

form of personal pleasure but spawn destructive and reckless public behavior, James M. Kouzes and Barry Z. Posner write:

> You cannot lead others until you have first led yourself through a struggle with opposing values. When you clarify the principles that will govern your life and the ends that you will seek, you give purpose to your daily decisions.

Kouzes and Posner continue:

> The internal resolution of competing beliefs also leads to personal integrity. And personal integrity is essential to believability. A leader with integrity has one self, at home and at work, with family and with colleagues. He or she has a unifying set of values that guide choices of action regardless of the situation.[3]

MAKING THE CONNECTION

If we are ever going to reestablish the crucial connection between personal character and public performance when it comes to the area of leadership, it will have to begin with a clear understanding of the fundamental role the development of personal values plays in the making of a leader. Since private, personal values are so instrumental in determining a leader's public behavior, it becomes essential that leaders be able to clearly define and identify their personal values.

In the most basic sense, values are those things to which we attach a relative worth, utility, or importance. Personal values, then, are the different concepts, ideas, principles, and things to which an individual attributes worth, utility, or importance. When I speak of personal values, I am not suggesting that they are tantamount to or synonymous with moral absolutes or ultimate right and wrong. Our personal values may or may not reflect moral absolutes and ultimate right and wrong. However, the more closely aligned our personal values are with what is widely held to be moral absolutes and ultimate right and wrong, the greater the likelihood that our public behavior will not create significant problems for us in our exercise of leadership and life in general.

For example, I place a high value on my personal appearance. The worth, utility, and importance I place on being physically fit, well-groomed, and fashionably attired is relatively high. As a result, this personal value drives a significant amount of my behavior. I work out regularly. I shower and shave daily. I keep my hair as well-groomed as is possible for the straight and non-cooperative locks inherited from the Native American branch of my family. And I try to make sure my suits have the proper number of buttons (not an easy task, considering twenty-first-century fashion) and that my ties are not too wide or too narrow. Proper appearance is one of the many personal values I hold. Now this particular value has virtually nothing to do with any moral absolutes or issues of ultimate right and wrong yet it remains for me an important value.

The question is not whether all of our personal values represent moral absolutes, but whether moral absolutes and issues of intrinsic value are well represented on the menu of our personal values. Furthermore, it is important that moral absolutes ultimately take precedence over personal values when a values conflict exists.

As a committed Christian, one of the values in my personal constitution is: "I will maintain a growing and increasingly intimate conversational relationship with God." My personal creed goes on to state:

> The single most vital and important value I hold is a personal belief in a living, loving, personal, sovereign God. This God desires to know me and interact with me. I will be conscious of my relationship with God and place it above every other value, priority, or goal. I will avoid every influence and activity that undermines my relationship with God.[4]

Obviously this stated value is closely aligned with what I believe to be an absolute. But there are other values, such as my value to "Always see things as they can be, not simply as they are," that are less obviously aligned with any moral absolute. We all have values regarding things like personal pleasure, finances and money, relationships, personal success and accomplishment, family, and countless other things, not all of which deal directly with absolutes. And yet, for us, they are still values that we hold.

Where Our Values Come From

My grandfather came of age during the worst years of the Great Depression. He lived on the Spokane Indian Reservation in northeast Washington state and eked out an existence for his family of nine by doing whatever he could that would produce a few bucks. It was not an easy life, and it was during these years that my grandfather began to value frugality and "making do" with what he had. Not surprisingly, then, one of my grandfather's highest personal values was scrimping and stretching everything in an effort to make it last. It's to be expected that this value impacted his personal behavior. I can't remember a time when I visited my grandfather's house that he wasn't deeply involved in some salvage project. He would sit in his chair and visit with us as he resoled his ancient shoes or sewed new patches on the elbows of his one sport coat. After his death, it was discovered that my grandfather left behind money that he had squirreled away in asbestos-lined coffee cans carefully hidden in the basement of his house and the backyard. Apparently, because of his experiences during the depression, my grandfather didn't place a very high value on banks and other financial institutions.

My grandfather's behavior puzzled me as a child. I always wondered as we sat in that small living room, overcrowded as it was with secondhand, cobbled together furniture, why Grandpa always seemed to be fixing something old. I remember asking my dad, "Why is Grandpa like that?" At the time my dad could not give me any clear answers that a kid my age could comprehend. Instead, Dad simply said, "That's just how Grandpa is."

My dad's answer was accurate as far as it went. That was just the way my grandpa was. But now I have a better understanding of *why* he was like he was. His odd behaviors were driven by deeply held personal values that were forged in the crucible of the Great Depression.

The same is true for each of us when it comes to the development and evolution of our own personal values. The values we hold today have been shaped by our past experiences and the environment in which we grew up. If we grew up in church where there was an emphasis on God and spirituality, then that has no doubt had an influence on what we value today—whether our values are consistent with what we were exposed to or whether our current values reflect a rejection of those early influences.

For people who grew up in an austere home environment, while at the same time being exposed to other families who enjoyed an abundance of material wealth, avoiding poverty and pursuing a more comfortable lifestyle might, understandably, become a personal value.

Regardless of the shape our present values have taken, they have been influenced by the experiences of our past.

THE ROLE OF VALUES IN LEADERSHIP

No matter what their origin, as we have seen, our personal values will inevitably influence our behavior. Thus it is essential as leaders that we be able to clearly identify and articulate our unique values. Only then will we know if they align with those of the organization we lead. Whether we exercise leadership as a pastor in the local church environment, an executive in a parachurch ministry, a manager in a Christian business, an administrator in a school, a denominational leader, or in some other venue, leaders are expected to personally model to some degree the values of the organization they serve. According to Aubrey Malphurs:

> The leader's actions clearly demonstrate and reinforce the values that he or she believes to be important—the high-priority values. Every organization has numerous beliefs, and the leader's behavior indicates which are the more important ones. This is why it is so crucial that the leader have ownership of the ministry's values set and be willing to commit to them. A lack of ownership means that the leader will follow a values set different from the organization's stated values. *The result will be chaos, disruption, and the potential demise of the organization.*[5]

This is what we witnessed as a nation during Clinton's presidency. The incongruity between President Clinton's personal values and the values of the organization (the United States government) led to a period of political chaos, uncertainty, and disruption. Previously unknown to many, certain personal values that President Clinton demonstrated by his behavior were in direct conflict with what the majority of Americans deem to be important values for the effective functioning of our government. For example, it was demonstrated beyond all dispute that the president places a high personal value on satisfying certain physical urges. Time and time again, not just on isolated occasions but routinely over a period of years, this value took precedence over other values, such as faithfulness and circumspection—values that are essential to the running of our country.

To exacerbate the problem, the president's personal values of self-preservation and image produced a steady stream of subtle deceptions and even outright lies. Again we see that the president's personal values were at odds with what most people would consider fundamental values, namely, honesty and truthfulness.

This same dynamic can be true for any leader in any organization. That is why identifying, articulating, and then embracing one's personal values is so absolutely foundational to the exercise of healthy, effective leadership in any organization or leadership environment. By doing so, the leader minimizes the potential for chaos, disruption, and even the possible demise of the organization that can result when there exists a conflict between the values of the leader and those of the organization to which she is giving leadership.

Though identifying, articulating, and embracing your personal values may seem like a simple process, few tasks will require a leader to make such a concentrated effort in focused contemplation, reflection, and personal examination than this one. But challenging and time-consuming as it may be, it is absolutely essential for effective, healthy, long-term leadership.

The strong temptation for most leaders is to simply begin leading. After all, that's what leaders do. However, an effective leader must make a well-informed choice of what type of organization is the best fit for him. And that can be done only with a solid grasp of the personal values he owns.

LAYING THE FOUNDATION

So where do we begin in our efforts to identify and articulate our personal values in such a way that we can then boldly and unwaveringly embrace them? This important process, which will provide a sure foundation for our leadership, actually involves three essential steps. Step one is to take the time to actually discover our basic personal values. Step two involves giving further definition to the values we have identified, and, finally, step three requires that we begin living our life and practicing our leadership with our articulated values clearly in mind.

STEP ONE: IDENTIFYING OUR VALUES

How do we go about the task of identifying our values? It seems that for many leaders the area of personal values is one of those areas in life that is often taken for granted. If asked, we'd be quick to say, "Sure I have values I live by," yet at the same time we would be hard-pressed to give any kind of concrete shape to them or articulate a concise definition.

The best and most troubling place to begin when it comes to identifying our values is to explore our present behavior. If, in fact, our behavior is driven in large measure by our personal values, examining our usual behaviors is a good place to begin. It is important to remember as we engage in this process that it is very likely, in fact quite probable, that we will not like some of the values that we identify. Some of the values we begin to uncover will be values we want to change. That's good. The reality is that before we can ever change our less admirable values, we must clearly identify them. Thus we must resist the temptation to ignore and rationalize the more unappealing values that have been driving some of our behaviors up to this point. Now is the time to make any changes you may deem beneficial to your life and the exercise of your leadership.

So how exactly do we examine our behaviors and understand how they reflect or reveal our values? Though the specifics will be different for all of us, the process will be quite similar for everyone. For example, if a common behavior for you is compulsive spending, you need to ask yourself what has such high value for you that it causes you to regularly engage in this behavior. Could it be that you place a high value on the personal pleasure you feel from the immediate gratification engendered by compulsive spending? If so, it may be that you place a high personal value on pleasure. At the same time, it could be that the compulsive spending is driven by the value of personal freedom—the ability to enjoy the freedom of purchasing a particular item at the time you want it. Or it may be driven by feelings of low self-worth or poor self-image. You value the way purchasing expensive items makes you feel better about yourself.

Obviously the same behavior in three different people could be driven by three entirely different personal values. Only you can determine what particular value is driving your behavior in certain areas. This identification process will require a good deal of thought and a degree of honesty, transparency, and sobriety if it is to be at all helpful and constructive. Unfortunately many leaders simply are not willing to invest the time and do the self-investigation that this process requires.

Here are other examples. If a frequent behavior for you is maintaining the practice of regular spiritual disciplines, what is the value you hold that is fueling that practice? Is it that you place a high value on God and developing a personal relationship with him? Or could it be that your behavior is being driven by a need to maintain a sense of personal order? Could it be possible that your practice of spiritual disciplines is being driven by a combination of these values? If you engage in regular physical exercise, is your exercise motivated by the value you place on your health or is it motivated primarily by the value you place on your appearance?

To review, step one involves simply listing the various behaviors in which you regularly engage (unflattering as some of them may be). At the end of your personal exploration in step one, you should end up with a list of values similar to the one below:

MY BASIC VALUES

God

Personal Health

Family

Financial Responsibility

Appearance

Truth

Honesty

Recreation

Relationships

Although this is by no means an exhaustive list, it represents an idea of what some basic values might look like once identified. When this is complete, we must then take the next step of defining these values in a more articulate manner.

STEP TWO: DEFINING AND ARTICULATING OUR VALUES

Using the list that you created in the previous step, it is time to give thought to developing a more thorough definition for each of these basic values. This should involve writing a concise but thorough definition of what we specifically mean when we say that we value God or personal health, for instance. Following the expanded definition, we write briefly about how we respond to or would like to respond to that value. For example, one of the values in my personal constitution states: "I value my physical health, fitness, and appearance."

I then go on to give a more thorough definition and my response to this particular value:

My body is the temple of the Holy Spirit of the living God and my only vehicle for accomplishing all that God desires me to accomplish. Because I value my health, fitness, and appearance,

45

I will maintain self-control in my eating habits. I will exercise my body at least five times a week and keep my weight under 180 pounds at all times. I will always give special attention to my personal appearance and look the best I possibly can so that my appearance in no way impedes the successful accomplishment of the mission to which God has called me.

When we say that we value our family, what exactly does that mean to us? It is vital that we be able to articulate our values, give them specific definition, and think about our response to them. As we then regularly review the definitions of our values, they begin to become a conscious part of us and more consistently inform our activities and decisions.

As I reviewed my regular behaviors, I found that I spend a lot of time involved in activities related to the church. I preach and teach; I serve on boards and committees; I interact with many different people in the church both recreationally and for ministry purposes. Thus I identified the church as one of my basic values and further defined this basic value in my personal constitution:

> Because I value the church I will contribute to its growth, and through it the advancement of God's kingdom, by promoting and developing healthy leaders who can serve within the church. The church is not just an organization but a community united around the person and work of Jesus Christ. It is the single most important and influential force in the world. Society and culture prosper to the degree that the church of Jesus Christ is growing and healthy.

As previously mentioned, not all of our goals will be as lofty and positive as the ones just articulated. The sobering reality is that some of our current values will be quite negative and destructive. For example, one of the negative values I mentioned earlier was compulsive spending. The defined value might look something like this:

> Because I place a high value on what others think of me and have an unhealthy need for the approval and acceptance of others, I engage in compulsive spending for things I don't need. Often I do this by using credit cards that I cannot fully pay off by the end of the month, thus crippling me with unnecessary debt.

The purpose of this exercise is to force us to engage in the some-times painful process of thinking deeply about the values that drive our behavior. Often we are conscious of these values at some level but have never taken the time to articulate them. At the same time, we are often aware of destructive behaviors we engage in but have never stopped to fully consider the deeply held values that are driving them. This exercise can help bring some clarity to our behaviors as well as to the values that are behind them. Before we can ever proactively engage in effective self-leadership, we must become very conscious of our values in this way.

Another set of values we need to articulate is those values we wish we possessed but as yet do not. It is in step three that we should take the time to survey our identified values and add to the list any desired values that are not yet a part of our life.

For each of the values we list, we need to develop a defini-tion. Once this is complete, it is time to move to the final step in the process.

STEP THREE: EMBRACING OUR VALUES

Once we have identified and then articulated our values in a comprehensive written description, we must begin to fully embrace the positive ones. Simply to identify and define our values will be only moderately helpful unless we decide to embrace them fully.

To embrace something means to adopt it or to include it in our daily practice of life and leadership. Our values should begin to encircle every decision we make and every action we take. When that happens, we will begin to live a truly value-driven life and provide value-driven leadership to the organizations we are privileged to lead.

Though it is true that the values we have identified are already a part of our behavior in some way (that is how we arrived at them after all), that in no way assumes that we are consciously and proactively leading our life by them and using them as guid-ing principles. I eat, but it does not necessarily follow that I am consciously eating with the purpose of fueling my body for healthy living. I may make time for personal spiritual disciplines, but that does not mean that I can articulate exactly why I do them and how they contribute to my effective self-leadership. That is why it is important to distill our values into brief statements so that we can keep them before us daily and consciously utilize them to give direction to our life.

It is also important to keep our negative values before us—with the purpose of changing them. I recommend adding a prescriptive action to the end of each negative value that will move us in the direction of replacing the negative value with a positive one, which fosters constructive behaviors. For example, adding a prescriptive action to our previously identified negative value of compulsive spending could look like this:

> Because I place a high value on what others think of me and have an unhealthy need for the approval and acceptance of others, I engage in compulsive spending for things I don't need. Often I do this by using credit cards that I cannot fully pay off by the end of the month, thus crippling me with unnecessary debt.
>
> *But because I am fully accepted and approved by God, I need to resist the temptation to define my worth and value by the material things I possess. I will not purchase things I do not need in the vain attempt to gain the approval of others.*

THE DECISION OF A VALUE-DRIVEN LEADER

When a leader is guided by deeply held personal values, those values will permeate the decisions he makes and the leadership he provides and will add value to the organization and all that it does.

On December 11, 1995, fire destroyed the Malden Mills Textile Factory in Lawrence, Massachusetts, employer of more than 400 workers. The mill, owned by Aaron Feurestein, which had been in operation for ninety years, had been reduced to a heap of charred rubble. Many of the employees feared that the only course of action their leader could take would be to collect the insurance money and close the mill. They knew that rebuilding and updating the old mill would be extremely expensive. But contrary to everyone's fears and much to their surprise, Aaron Feurestein made the decision not to close the factory—but to rebuild. An even more staggering decision Mr. Feurestein made was to continue paying his employees their salary and benefits—a sum of $1.5 million a week—until the mill was reopened.

It was a decision that was applauded by the entire nation and even caused President Clinton to call to express his admiration and invite Feurestein to the State of the Union address as his personal guest. As he was lauded for his exceptional actions this leader responded by saying, "What? For doing the decent thing?"

You see, this was the only decision that Feurestein could make, based on his deeply held personal values. He was brought up to believe that a leader who provides for others has a moral responsibility to do so in good times as well as bad. In explanation of his decision he quoted the ancient Jewish Rabbi Hillel, who said, "In a place where there's moral depravity and no feeling of moral responsibility, do your best to be a man." His value-driven leadership had produced a decision of value, even at great personal cost, and that decision has resulted in an amazing resurgence for Malden Mills as they've taken the lead in producing the space-age fabric Polartec. In addition, Aaron Feurestein has created a work environment in which many of his employees would literally lay down their lives for their leader.

Leaders who lead lives that are guided by unwavering, deeply held personal values will make decisions of value that will greatly enhance all that they do.

A SELF-LEADERSHIP WORKSHOP

For help in implementing the steps that have been discussed in this chapter, use the following exercises that guide you through this process.

IDENTIFYING YOUR LIFE'S VALUES

Take some time in a quiet place to begin reflecting on the behaviors that you engage in on a regular basis. What are those things that you are most involved in and passionate about? At the same time, think of those behaviors that have become a regular part of your life that you do not necessarily feel are all that positive. If you have kept a personal journal or diary for an extended period of time, now would be a good time to reread significant portions of it as an aid to your reflection.

As you begin to isolate some of your regular behaviors, record them in the left-hand column of the grid provided below. For example, if one of your regular behaviors is daily exercise, write that in the left column under "Behavior."

Behavior	Personal Value That Drives the Behavior

Now that you have isolated some of your regular behaviors and activities, it is important to identify the values that are driving those activities and behaviors. Again, this will require a degree of honesty and reflection that at first attempt might seem awkward and forced. However, this is a vital part of the process. To review how this is to be done, turn back to Step One: Identifying Our Values in this chapter and reread the section.

Now, in a concise statement of one to five words, write in the right column of the grid the value that you feel is driving each behavior you listed. For example, for daily exercise, the value may be: Concern for health and appearance. If you listed daily spiritual disciplines under "Behavior," the personal value may be: Personal relationship with God.

ARTICULATING YOUR VALUES

Now it is time to give a more specific and detailed definition to the basic values you have listed. For each basic value you have identified, take some time to write out a brief, yet comprehensive, paragraph that defines what you mean. For example, if you identified "Concern for health and appearance" as one of your values, go on to give a more thorough definition of this particular value. You may write something like I did:

> My body is the temple of the Holy Spirit of the living God and my only vehicle for accomplishing all that God desires me to accomplish. Because I value my health, fitness, and appearance, I will maintain self-control in my eating habits. I will exercise my body at least five times a week and keep my weight under 180 pounds at all times. I will always give special attention to my personal appearance and look the best I possibly can so that my appearance in no way impedes the successful accomplishment of the mission to which God has called me.

Do this for each of the basic values you have listed. By doing so, you are creating the essential building blocks that you will use to construct your own Personal Constitution, which is a document that articulates your governing values and which you will take time to read on a daily or weekly basis once it is complete. In the space provided below, write your values definitions.

51

Value:

Definition:

Value:

Definition:

Value:

Definition:

Value:

Definition:

Value:
Definition:

Value:
Definition:

Value:
Definition:

Value:
Definition:

With this renewed understanding of our life values, it is time to turn our attention to the second foundational issue in self-leadership: connecting with our Calling.

3

CONNECTING WITH YOUR LIFE'S CALLING

Just as our personal values will dictate in large measure our actions and behavior, a strong connection with our sense of Calling is what will give a degree of purpose and overall direction to our actions. The nineteenth-century Scottish historian and essayist Thomas Carlyle said, "There is nothing more terrible than activity without insight." To extend Carlyle's statement a bit further, I believe it is safe to say that anyone who desires to be an effective leader must consistently engage in activity that is not only informed by insight but is also generated by a strong inner sense of purpose or Calling.

To effectively master the art of self-leadership, a person must develop a strong connection with a sense of calling that guides his actions and elevates his daily activity above the mundane, imbuing all efforts with an intrinsic, metaphysical value.

A CEO CONNECTS WITH HIS CALLING

At fifty-two Bruce Kennedy was the chief executive officer of the highly successful Alaska Air Group, the parent company of Alaska Airlines. During twelve years under Kennedy's leadership, the corporation's revenues grew tenfold. When he took the helm the airline was floundering and nearly bankrupt. But in those twelve years he brought transformation to the organization and saw it become one of the most profitable and best-run airlines in the entire world. Then, at the peak of his success, he made a shocking decision. He stepped down from his lofty corporate position to become the board chairman of the Redlands, California–based Mission Aviation Fellowship, an international Christian organization that specializes in flying missionaries to remote locations. Kennedy's new position has no salary at all; he is a volunteer.

Though Bruce Kennedy is quick to admit that his was a scary decision, it was also a decision that was driven by a clear inner sense of Calling. After ten years as the CEO he decided he wanted to spend the rest of his life doing what God wanted him to do. "If I say that I trust God and put my life in his hands—if it's as I've said it is—then I shouldn't have any reservations about proving it with my life," the leader said.[1]

In an effort to more fully determine what God was calling him to, he and his wife applied to experiment in several different mission settings, including working with Mother Teresa. Explaining his rationale, Kennedy said, "In one year, there are four major endeavors to find out what's going on in the world. . . . I feel confident that we will get a clear nudging (from God) to do some particular work in due course."

Not only is Bruce Kennedy a leader with deeply held personal values that have shaped his life practices, he is also a leader who is intent on allowing a clear sense of Calling to give direction to his future activity.

Though Kennedy left Alaska Air Group to further flesh out his Calling, he had used his position in the company as a theater for acting out his Calling in the business world. He says, "I have no sense that it's God's will to profit companies—I think God deals in relationships with individuals, not prospering businesses. Perhaps in prospering this business, he has done something to teach people his ways." Whether leading a multinational corporation or serving full-time with Mother Teresa in Calcutta, Bruce Kennedy is a leader who leads his life out of a deep inner sense of Calling that gives purpose and meaning to all he does. For him it is not his position that gives value and purpose to his life, but rather it is his life's Calling that gives purpose and value to his positions, whatever or wherever they may be.

WHAT IS A CALLING?

If we are to connect with our life's Calling, it is vital that we be able to make a clear distinction between *Calling* with a capital *c* and *calling* with a lowercase *c*.

According to pastor and author Ben Patterson, our Calling (capital *c*) has to do with our vocation in life.[2] Unfortunately in today's career-obsessed world, many people associate vocation with their career. In other words, their vocation is what they do in life professionally or the work they engage in at their job. Today if someone were to inquire as to our vocation, we would likely respond by saying that we are a stockbroker or a physician. This use, however, does not accurately represent the true and original meaning of the word. Vocation comes from the Latin word *vocare,* which literally means, "to call."[3] Originally a person's vocation was her life's Calling, which transcends any particular job or professional career. The New Testament Greek word that has the same meaning as the Latin *vocare* is the word *kaleo,* which also means "to call" or "to summon."[4] In Galatians, when Paul seeks to explain to the Galatians the radical change that transformed him from his vocation as a Pharisee to that of an apostle of Christ, it is the word *kaleo* that he uses. Paul says, "But then something happened! For it pleased God in his kindness to choose me and call *(kaleo)* me, even before I was born!" (Gal. 1:15). In Ephesians 4, as Paul writes to encourage these believers who were immersed in an incredibly pagan and secular culture, he reminds them of their vocation as Christians. Paul implores the Ephesians to "lead a life worthy of your calling *(kaleo)*, for you have been called *(kaleo)* by God" (Eph. 4:1). Yet again, a few sentences later, in this letter to beloved fellow believers Paul writes, "We are all one body, we have the same Spirit, and we have all been called *(kaleo)* to the same glorious future" (v. 4).

For the apostle Paul there was only one Calling for those who proclaim the name of Christ—and that was the transcendent, metaphysical reality that all who profess faith in Christ are first and foremost children of God. Christian leaders have but one vocation, or Calling, in this life and that is as members of the same universal body of Jesus Christ. As leaders we are all called to the same glorious future—exercising our leadership as a means to the same end. We have been called to be citizens of a different kingdom (Phil. 3:20).

The apostle Peter clearly concurs with Paul's understanding of our vocation as Christians when he writes,

> But you are not like that [people without a sense of purpose or being], for you are a chosen people. You are a kingdom of priests, God's holy nation, and his very own possession. This is so you can show others the goodness of God, for he called you out of the darkness into his wonderful light.
>
> 1 Peter 2:9

Again and again throughout the pages of Scripture we are reminded that our Calling as people far exceeds in importance and purpose any possible job or career in which we might engage, regardless of the status given to it by our particular society. Our vocation as Christian leaders, no matter what the environment in which we exercise our leadership, is to be a holy nation, a royal priesthood, God's own special possession. Our Calling is to be reflectors of the wonderful light of God so that it will illumine the path of others and guide them to hear, understand, and respond to the Calling that God may be issuing to them as well. That is the very essence of our leadership. In fact connecting with the reality of our Calling in a meaningful way is the key that will unlock for us a life of enduring significance and purpose that informs every other activity in which we engage.

A physician friend of mine, who also attends my church, is the head of the pediatric department at the University of South Dakota Medical School, which also serves a large regional hospital. Larry is a highly respected educator and physician who is currently in the prime of his career. Though he could have his pick of prestigious positions throughout the country, he chooses to stay in his current position. The reason? It has become for him an excellent platform from which he exercises his true Calling. On my recent visit to the hospital that also included a tour of his department, virtually every room we entered sparked in him a memory of a family he had consoled, an occasion on which he was able to share his faith, or an opportunity he had to pray with a grieving or frightened parent. As he shared these stories with me, I was somewhat surprised. "Can you do that? Can you actually pray with people right here in their room?" I asked.

Larry looked at me rather incredulously, no doubt surprised that a minister would ask such a stupid question, and simply responded, "Of course!" You see, Larry has connected with his life's true Calling. He is aware that he is not merely a physician caring for the physical needs of his patients but also a follower of Christ who has been called to a much larger vocation. Larry has led numerous people to faith in Christ in his role as a physician. He is not apologetic about what some would label an inappropriate mixing of medicine and religion because he recognizes that his primary Calling in life is to be a healer of souls. The practice of medicine is simply the platform from which he exercises that Calling. As a result, Larry is fulfilled and seems to thoroughly enjoy his life and work.

It is only as we connect with our Calling, or true vocation, that we can find meaning and transcendent fulfillment in our calling (lowercase *c*). For our purposes in this book, a calling refers to our avocation or, as Webster describes it, "A *subordinate* occupation pursued in addition to one's vocation" (emphasis mine). A small-*c* calling refers to customary, ordinary employment. You see, ideally, our calling or occupation is to be exercised in subordination to our true, transcendent Calling in life that can be only spiritual in nature. That is what my friend Larry has done. His avocation as a physician is subordinate to his Calling as a healer of souls.

The tragedy today is that too many leaders, both Christian and non-Christian, have sold their vocational birthright for a bowl of avocational porridge. Then we wonder why our life's work is so shallow, banal, and unable to inspire us to greatness. We have become a culture searching for our vocation or true Calling in our work or careers, rather than allowing our true Calling to elevate our everyday work to the place where it becomes simply another platform on which we live out our vocation. Until we are able to make this necessary shift in our paradigm, we will never be able to lead our own life in a meaningful way, let alone lead other individuals or an organization. Mastering the art of self-leadership demands that we make this connection with our Calling and allow it to serve as the guiding force for all of our activities, whether they are related to our occupation or the everyday living of life. It was Bruce Kennedy's connection with his true vocation that enabled him to find purpose and meaning in whatever he did. It was his connection with his Calling that allowed him to leave a highly lucrative subordinate occupation to exercise his leadership in other ways, through other occupations. Bruce Kennedy knew that he could enjoy many callings, based on his gifts, experience, and knowledge, but his commitment is that every calling be used to flesh out his one true Calling.

ONE CALLING

The reality is that many leaders will probably experience many different occupations during their lifetime. There are many different organizations and causes that can benefit from gifted leadership and can provide a worthy platform from which we can exercise our leadership. However, we must realize that everything we do must be done in a way that enables us to further our true Calling in life. We can't lose sight of the forest for the trees!

I submit that we cannot even make a wise decision regarding our occupation or the environment in which we can best exercise our leadership until we are firmly convinced of and fully embrace our Calling.

One of the reasons that we see so many leadership failures and leaders who are desperately clinging to their occupations and organizational positions long after they have ceased to be truly effective is because these leaders have no clear sense of inner Calling. They think they can give definition and transcendent purpose to their life by virtue of the position they hold. But the reverse is true. When we connect with our life's true Calling, we can exercise meaningful, purposeful leadership regardless of the occupation in which we work.

Transcendent Meaning While Making Tents

The apostle Paul was a leader who finally connected with his life's true Calling after many years of pursuing meaning and purpose in a socially esteemed occupation. Paul ultimately discovered his life's Calling as a follower of Christ and was able to find a transcendent purpose for his life even as a humble tent maker. How paradoxical! As a Pharisee among Pharisees, a well-educated and socially connected religious leader, Saul of Tarsus led a miserable and destructive life. As an itinerant tent maker he led a life of purpose and he exercised leadership that literally changed the face of our planet for the better. It is doubtful that there is a single person alive today who has not in some way been affected by this self-employed tent maker. In fact, because Paul clearly understood his life's Calling and the future he was inexorably moving toward, he could confidently say:

> for I have learned how to get along happily whether I have much or little. I know how to live on almost nothing or with everything. I have learned the secret of living in every situation, whether it is with a full stomach or empty, with plenty or little.
>
> Philippians 4:11–12

When, like the apostle Paul, we have connected with our life's Calling, we will be able to exercise meaningful, transcendent leadership that has the potential of influencing the world regardless of our occupation. This connecting with our calling is an essential element of self-leadership.

AVOCATION AS A VEHICLE

In my research I have read many books that are promoted as tools to help the reader connect with his life's Calling in such a way as to produce a sense of genuine fulfillment. Unfortunately none of the books I have read are able to deliver on their lofty promises. The reality is that these books are designed to help the reader discover the avocation or occupation that is best suited to her, assuming that once that occupation is discovered, the pieces of life will fall into place. In other words, these authors promote the philosophy that the purpose of our existence on this planet is somehow related to finding just the right job or the career that best utilizes our gifts and enables us to give expression to our inner self.

The sad truth is that there are countless people who have found the perfect career or avocation for themselves and are still restlessly in pursuit of some transcendent purpose or reason for their existence. Whether they are Pulitzer prize-winning writers, Oscar-adorned actors, wealthy financiers, or fantastically creative architects, many of these people have been left wondering out loud "Is this all there is?" And yet, paradoxically, there are everyday bricklayers, schoolteachers, housewives, and, yes, even sanitation engineers, who have discovered a deep inner sense of purpose that gives meaning to whatever position they hold and any avocation in which they are involved.

This chapter is not in any way intended to suggest that our calling or avocation should be diminished in its importance or value. On the contrary, it is, in fact, exceedingly valuable and important when it is rightly understood and utilized as the vehicle through which we live out our life's true Calling, rather than expecting it to be the source of our life's Calling and our reason for existing. We need to realize that there are likely numerous avocations and occupations that will enable us to effectively live out our Calling. And yet it is true that there are probably a select few avocations that will provide for us a special fit between our Calling and career. Thus finding the right avocation is important. Though it is true that we can live out our Calling and find transcendent purpose in any occupation, it is also true that some occupations will allow us to make an even greater contribution to God's kingdom work.

FOLLOWING THE CLUES

So how do we actually go about determining what avocation(s) will provide the best platform from which we can most effectively live out our Calling? I would like to suggest a series of clues that you can follow that may lead you to just the right avocation for you. As you look for the best occupation, you need to consider such things as your previous experiences, present circumstances, possible opportunities, personal gifts, the prompting of the Holy Spirit, your personal passions, and the wisdom of private counsel. Though I am sure there are many clues I have not included here, these will certainly provide a good place to begin the process.

PREVIOUS EXPERIENCES

I remember struggling while in seminary to discover which discipline within the ministry I should pursue. For a couple of years I vacillated between counseling, teaching, becoming a pastor, or even possibly a missionary. After one particularly riveting presentation by a Wycliffe Bible translator during a chapel service, I felt certain that I should become a Bible translator in some remote South American jungle. Surely that would be important and valuable work. I remember discussing the possibility with one of my professors, who seemed to find it odd that I would be interested in such a path based on what he knew about my wife and me. In an effort to bring some clarity to my thinking, he began to ask me a series of questions. "Sam, have you ever been to a foreign country?" he inquired. "No," I replied. "Have you ever been on a short-term mission in the States?" he probed further. "Nope." He continued, "Do you speak any foreign languages?" "Not yet, but I can learn," I responded. "Has your wife ever been on a mission or to a foreign country?" he wanted to know. "No . . ." I hesitated, beginning to see where this was headed. "Sam, does your wife like to camp and live in the wild?" I had to admit that my wife had never been camping in her life. Finally, he asked one more question. "Sam, what makes you think that God is calling you to be a Bible translator in the deepest jungles of South America?" I didn't have much of an answer for him and by this time felt somewhat silly.

What my professor was delicately trying to help me see was that based on my previous experiences, or should I say lack of experiences in this instance, there was really no reason I should pursue the avocation of a Bible translator. This is not to say that I could not have been a successful translator. However, it did mean that I had a significant amount of experience to gain at a relatively late date.

At the same time, when it comes to ministry, I have been reminded that often God can give us a deep desire to engage in a ministry for which we have had no preparatory experiences. In these cases our deep desire has been given to us by God to point us in the direction of the work he has already gifted us for. In such cases it could be that the necessary gifts for such a ministry have been dormant and our desire, kindled by God, could be a clue for the new direction in which he wants us to move.

Often our previous life experiences will provide some clues to the occupation that will provide the best platform for us. Again, this is not to say that we cannot gain the necessary experience to pursue a path that we have not already been experientially prepared for. It simply means that there may not be an immediate connection with some possible avocations, the pursuit of which would require some additional time.

For example, if you have never done well in math and have had little experience in accounting and bookkeeping, those could be clues that becoming a CPA is not the most realistic career choice. If you have always struggled with writing and have never really written anything other than a few letters here and there, your experiences may be providing a clue concerning your avocation, if you are willing to be sensitive.

The point is that our previous life experiences, or lack of them, can provide us with important clues when it comes to finding the avocation that will provide the best platform from which to live out our true Calling.

PRESENT CIRCUMSTANCES

I have a friend who is an amazingly gifted and skilled leader. He has exercised effective transformational leadership in many different venues and enjoys it immensely. He has tremendous experience in the business world as a top-level executive who has restructured corporate divisions and implemented significant organizational change. He holds a Ph.D. in business communication from a Big Ten university and enjoys countless contacts in the business community. However, at the present time, my friend is extremely unhappy in his current avocation. Though he occupies a prestigious position at a regional university that is well thought of in the community, it is clearly outside of his primary area of expertise. He is at a point in his life when he would love nothing more than to go into business for himself as a consultant to corporate clients. His children have completed college. His personal financial resources are sound and well managed. His wife is supportive of his desire to launch out on his own, and certain events have taken place at his present job to make the time seem right to strike out on a new avocational course.

For years it has been a dream, but the time just never seemed right and the risks of failure too consequential for a young family. But present circumstances have changed! It could be a clue that there is a different occupation out there that will allow my friend to have an even greater impact and effectively live out his life's Calling as a follower of Christ. An important clue that should never be overlooked when attempting to discover the best avocation for us involves a thorough examination of our present circumstances.

POSSIBLE OPPORTUNITIES

Yet another important clue that can provide us with direction involves the possible opportunities we have or that we see on the horizon of our life. When confronted with an opportunity, we can either affirm our present place and position or move in a new direction. Regardless of the decision we make, opportunities wisely assessed and dealt with can provide us with some invaluable clues that will keep us moving in the right direction.

When faced with an opportunity, it is important that we analyze it in light of our previous experiences as well as our present circumstances. Will the new opportunity enable us to utilize and build on previous experiences? Is it the answer to our present circumstances? Do our present circumstances allow us to take advantage of the opportunity in question with integrity?

Often, in our desire to do what we want, we attempt to create opportunities or force doors open that really should remain closed. That is why it is important to examine only those opportunities that are actually possible for us. Is the opportunity of running for political office a real one that can be successful or is it an opportunity that we are trying to create that has little likelihood of success? Is there a legitimate opportunity to open our own business or change professions, or would doing so be foolhardy and irresponsible? Is that inquiry from a new church a real opportunity, or something we have campaigned for and been personally active in orchestrating? These are some of the questions we need to ask as we determine the legitimacy of possible opportunities.

Often the opportunities that seem to come "out of the blue" or when we least expect them are genuine opportunities that warrant our close scrutiny. When an opportunity comes as a true serendipity, it may very well be that God is at work behind the scenes attempting to move us in a direction that will be better for us and make us more useful to him. Whether it is an opportunity that simply pops into our life or one that has been on the horizon for some time, each opportunity should be considered one more clue that God can use to lead us to the place he wants us.

PERSONAL GIFTS

One of the more obvious clues that will enable us to connect our life's true Calling with a fulfilling calling is our menu of personal gifts. Within this category I would include both our spiritual gifts and our natural talents.

This is not the appropriate place to provide a comprehensive discussion of spiritual gifts and the testing available to help uncover them. However, the better acquainted we are with our spiritual gifts, and the more finely tuned they are, the more likely they are to serve as a reliable clue for pointing us in the direction of a meaningful occupation that will serve as an effective platform from which we can live out our Calling.

This is also true when it comes to being familiar with our natural talents. The more we are aware of the talents we have, the better able we will be to find an occupation that can maximize them for God's glory. To help you explore the area of your gifts and natural talents, see the list of resources in appendix A.

PROMPTING OF THE HOLY SPIRIT

It is with rare exception that God does not provide us with meaningful direction and guidance at the critical junctures of our life. This is especially true when it comes to making important life decisions, such as determining what we will do in terms of an occupation.

The most important aspect of this clue is not whether the Holy Spirit of God prompts and guides us, but whether we are willing and able to discern his promptings when they come. All too often we fail to sense the Holy Spirit's guidance, either because we have predetermined the decision we will make or because we are too frantic and stressed to stop and hear the Spirit's still, quiet voice.

Though believers often feel uncertain and inadequate in discerning the prompting and direction of the Holy Spirit, I am convinced this is something at which we work much too hard.

When we sincerely want to know how God is directing us and are concerned with obeying and honoring him, we needn't worry that he won't communicate with us or that we will miss his direction.

In every major occupational decision I have made, and there have been some life-changing ones, I have always found that deep down I knew exactly what direction God was giving me. On some occasions I complicated things because I was afraid of the ramifications such direction might have on my life. At other times I didn't like what I was sensing and spent some time attempting to bargain with God and entice him into giving me what I wanted. Still other times I sensed an immediate response to what God was doing in my life, only to blur that initial response with needlessly convoluted and obsessive thinking on the issue. In most of those cases I have found that my final decision was the same as my initial response. But whatever I did to muddy the Spirit's directional waters at these confusing times, in the final analysis, if I am perfectly honest, there has always been an essentially clear understanding deep in my spirit of what I needed to do.

It is important for us to recognize, however, that the Spirit's prompting does not come exclusively as some warm inner burning or ethereal inner sense, though there is no disputing that God's promptings do take the form of inner urgings at times. He also will use all of the other clues presented here to help bring clarity and guidance.

Personal Passions

Another vital clue that can bring clarity to our search for a meaningful avocation from which we can live out our true Calling as a follower of Christ has to do with our personal passions. I am firmly convinced that God has given each of us unique passions for a very special and specific reason. When we are able to align our personal passions with both our education and occupation, we will have the best chance of finding that special avocation in which God can use us most effectively.

Our personal passions involve those issues, subjects, practices, and institutions for which we have an ardent affection. When we sense an intense, driving, almost overmastering concern in our life for a certain thing, it is likely that the object of that concern is for us a passion.

If I were to ask what the apostle Paul's passion was, most biblically literate people could identify his deep, driving concern for sharing the gospel of Jesus Christ with the Gentiles. Another passion we might identify would be his passion for expanding the church and ensuring its spiritual purity and health. These are obvious passions that drove the apostle Paul's life. On the other hand, if we were asked to identify King Solomon's passions, we would create an entirely different list: architecture, women, wealth, and possibly the search for a transcendent meaning for his life would likely find their way onto such a list.

I am convinced that we need to constantly ask ourselves what our passion is if we want to be in the most effective place of service that will allow us the greatest opportunity to live out our Calling and thus realize the most fulfillment and greatest sense of purpose. During the course of our spiritual and occupational journey it is probable that our passions will change or at least be refined and become more specific. What was a passion for us at age twenty-one may no longer be a passion at age fifty-five. Early in my ministry I was extremely passionate about personal counseling and enjoyed it very much. Now, fifteen years later, I no longer have the same passion for personal counseling. Instead, the same root issues that created a passion for individual counseling in my early ministry have now been broadened to the point where I feel a very similar passion for the congregation as a whole.

Too often we are willing to sell out our passion when it comes to finding an occupation in favor of money, prestige, or power, only to find a few years down the road that the money, prestige, and power we gained can never compensate for the passion we compromised.

Private Counsel

One final clue that we must be sensitive to in our search for the right avocation is the wise counsel of others more experienced and mature than we are. God can and will speak to us through wise counselors if we are willing to hear their message.

Very often, as we seek wise counsel in the decision-making process, the aggregate wisdom we receive will confirm what the other clues have been telling us.

It is important, however, that we not rely too heavily on only one or two counselors. We often have a tendency to seek out only the advice of those who we know will tell us what we want to hear. Better to approach a number of people we respect, share as objectively as possible the details of our situation, and then allow them to share with us their wisdom. My experience has been that though there probably will not be unanimity, a clear theme emerges that gives me some direction.

SEEING THE CLUES COME TOGETHER

What does it look like when all of these clues come together in a person's life? Obviously, the specifics will be different for each of us, but the general way they come together will be similar.

In the life of Moses we can see how all of these clues converged to bring clarity to what it was God was calling him to do. (See Exodus 2–4.) After a somewhat traumatic childhood in the house of Pharaoh and a hasty exit from Egypt as an adult wanted for murder, Moses ended up in the avocation of shepherd in the desert of Midian. There he spent forty years tending the sheep and herds of his father-in-law, Jethro. One day, without warning, Moses seemed to receive a challenge from God to change his avocation so that he could better live out his true Calling. God was not asking Moses to make just a minor transition.

As we review the familiar story, it is interesting to note how all six of the clues presented in this chapter converged to confirm what God was doing in the life of Moses.

Moses' *previous experiences* involved an intimate familiarity with Egyptian culture, which would be necessary for his new avocation. Moses also possessed an understanding of Egyptian politics at the highest levels and no doubt still had a few contacts. He was educated in Egyptian schools and understood the Egyptian mind-set. Much of his previous experience would be a great asset for the avocation to which God was calling him.

At the time this *opportunity* presents itself, Moses' *present circumstances* also seem to point in a specific direction. The Jews, Moses' people, were still in bondage, forced to do slave labor. They were crying out for a deliverer—the time was ripe for someone to fill the role of liberator for the people of Israel. And with God's promise of divine assistance and success, it was indeed a rare opportunity.

The *gifts* Moses possessed made him an understandable candidate for the job God had in mind as well. First, Moses was well educated. In fact he was probably the best-educated Jew alive at the time. Second, Moses was gifted in the ability to survive and scratch out an existence in the harsh desert climate, something he had demonstrated for the past forty years. This would certainly be no small prerequisite for the person assigned this task of liberation. It is doubtful there were any of the Egyptian captives who, after years of slavery, could even begin to rival Moses' skills in this area.

For Moses, the *divine prompting* would have been difficult to miss. God came to Moses in the form of the burning bush to extend this opportunity to him. Even though Moses wasn't too excited about the call he was receiving, it was well nigh impossible for him to explain away the bush and deny that it was God who spoke to him there.

One of the primary reasons Moses was tending sheep in the desert in the first place was his *passion* to see the Jews freed from their Egyptian slavery. So consuming was his passion that when he witnessed a Jewish laborer being mistreated, he killed the abuser. While his passion for the liberation of his people may have been kindled from afar during the past forty years of his life, God knew it wouldn't take much to fan it back to full flame.

Finally, Moses received confirmation in the form of *private counsel*. On hearing about this amazing opportunity, Moses' father-in-law, Jethro, didn't hesitate to give his blessing (4:18). In spite of the fact that Jethro probably had the most to lose in the proposition, he still encouraged Moses to follow this specific call of God.

In the life of Moses we can see how all of the clues came into alignment to lead Moses to make the occupational shift from shepherd to spokesman and leader.

71

DON'T EXPECT A BURNING BUSH

As I've already said, we can live out our true Calling through any avocation no matter how lofty or humble it may be. However, over time, as we exercise better and better self-leadership, we may begin to sense an inner urgency to find some avocation through which we can live out our Calling in a way that brings even greater kingdom effectiveness and personal fulfillment.

Obviously Moses had a greater impact advancing God's plan as a shepherd and leader of people than he probably would have had as a shepherd and leader of sheep. This is not to say that being a shepherd was not important. It was vitally important! It was only after forty years in Moses' avocation as a shepherd that God had fully prepared him to step into a new, more challenging avocation. We cannot be impatient in this process and must realize that the period of preparation is essential to the success of our future callings. When the time is right and God is ready for us, he will begin to give us the clues that will lead us to the new platform he has prepared for us.

Brian Proffit never saw any burning bushes, but God has called him to change his avocation just as convincingly as he called Moses.

Brian was a Christian but was more concerned with material matters than spiritual issues. Like many Christians who have been duped by our present culture, Brian was desperately trying to find a sense of transcendent purpose and meaning for his life through his avocation. By all standards, if anyone could find purpose and meaning in an avocation, Brian should have. As a systems engineer and designer of software for industry giant IBM, Brian was at the top of his occupational game. His expertise and success had led to exciting roles as the contributing editor and columnist for top computer industry magazines, as well as corporate labs director for the highly regarded journal *PC Week*. Brian had also honed his public presentation skills and was an accomplished public presenter, once addressing an audience of ten thousand people.

But Brian felt that he was drifting on a sea of misery and frustration. He simply had no inner peace or sense of purpose in his life. Brian says, "I had a six-figure salary and the title of director but I was miserable." Finally, in their search for peace and purpose, he and his wife decided to simplify their lives. They found a church in which they felt at home and began truly building their lives around God. It wasn't long before the things they once considered so important began to seem frivolous to them.

It was at that specific time Brian's pastor suggested the possibility that he consider attending seminary via the Internet as part of a new program being offered by Bethel Seminary in Saint Paul, Minnesota—an environment in which Brian would obviously feel very comfortable. Because of his strong gifts in oral and written communication and in light of his emerging passion for spiritual growth and the proclamation of God's Word, his pastor thought the timing was right. Slowly Brian began to see the clues lining up. He received confirmation and encouragement from friends and associates who knew him, and with that counsel Brian and his wife began the journey toward a new avocation at middle age.

Eventually Brian and his wife decided to leave their home in Florida to attend Bethel full-time and pursue pastoral ministry. Though Brian could have effectively lived out his Christian Calling as an IBM executive, God decided, for whatever reason, that Brian would be even more effective in his Calling if he had a different calling. There were no burning bushes or golden engraved announcements that heralded a new direction. But by following the clues, Brian was able to connect in a whole new way with his Calling and then connect his Calling with an entirely new calling that would provide an even more effective platform from which to minister in the name of Christ.

A Self-Leadership Workshop

For additional help in connecting with the best calling from which you can live out your Calling, work through the following exercises.

SHAPING YOUR AVOCATION

Take some time now to reflect and give shape to both your transcendent Calling or vocation as a follower of Christ and the avocation that will serve as the best platform from which you can live out your values and fulfill your Calling.

1. Using the material discussed on pages 57–61, articulate to the best of your ability what you perceive to be your transcendent Calling from God.

My Calling or Vocation

2. Now take some time to evaluate your present avocation in light of your transcendent Calling and the values you identified and articulated in the previous chapter's workshop section. (Identify your avocation not in terms of a title or position, but rather the essence of what it is you do in your present position.)

My Current Avocation

3. Understanding your present avocation, evaluate how well it serves as a platform from which you can live out your values and Calling.

After scoring each value, add together all the circled numbers, then divide by the number of values you listed. This is your rating. A rating of 5 or below may mean that you would benefit

My Calling:										
My Values	Degree to which current avocation serves as an effective platform from which to live out values and calling									
Value 1	Hinders me				Neither hinders nor facilitates			Facilitates me		
	1	2	3	4	5	6	7	8	9	10
Value 2	1	2	3	4	5	6	7	8	9	10
Value 3	1	2	3	4	5	6	7	8	9	10
Value 4	1	2	3	4	5	6	7	8	9	10
Value 5	1	2	3	4	5	6	7	8	9	10
Value 6	1	2	3	4	5	6	7	8	9	10

Total:

Rating:

from finding an avocation better suited to the living out of your values and Calling.

4. If you have a deep, abiding sense that some other avocation might serve as a better platform (that is consistent with your values) from which you can ultimately fulfill God's Calling for your life, take some time to reflect on the seven clues that lead to the best calling. Briefly list the pertinent information in regard to

75

what God has been doing in your life (review the section Following the Clues).

	What God has been doing in this area
Previous Experiences	
Present Circumstances	
Possible Opportunities	
Personal Gifts	
Prompting of the Holy Spirit	
Personal Passions	
Private Counsel	

5. If there were no obstacles (money, education, geography, etc.), what kind of position or career would you create for yourself? Write the elements of your ideal avocation in the space below.

My Ideal Avocation

6. What are some things you could do to make your ideal avocation a reality for you (for example, more education, networking, exploring opportunities, etc.)?

Making My Ideal Avocation a Reality
a.
b.
c.
d.
e.
f.
g.

4

LAYING OUT YOUR LIFE'S GOALS

Back in 1982 as my wife and I were desperately attempting to adjust to the frenzied, overwhelming life of seminary and at the same time anticipating the birth of our first child, we did something that, at the time, seemed quite strange to us. At a chapel service at *Insight for Living,* where I worked throughout my seminary years, I heard a rather compelling talk on the importance of having objective goals. When I got home that day, I told my wife, Sue, "We've got to set some goals!"

At the time we really had only two major goals and those were to survive our first year of seminary and experience the healthy birth of our first child. Frankly, I remember thinking that our plates were already pretty full—too full to load up with any additional, clearly extracurricular, new objectives or energetic goals. And yet at the same time I sensed a compelling need to sit down with Sue and spend some time together thinking and praying about what God might want some of our personal life goals as a newly married couple to be.

To this day, almost twenty years later, I can still remember the trepidation with which we sat at the banged-up kitchen table we had recently rescued from a garage sale. At the time, our entire monthly gross income as a couple (and it truly was gross!) was 800 dollars. The rent for our apartment alone was 350 dollars a month, and we could always count on there being more month than money every pay cycle. I drove a 1974, rusted-out, orange Toyota, which had recently migrated from the harsh cold of an Iowa winter with a fellow seminary student and which I was able to purchase for about a thousand dollars, paid with monthly installments over a period of one year. There was not a single piece of furniture in our apartment that had not been inherited from a family member or purchased secondhand. To put it more simply and straightforwardly, we were impoverished students who had just entered what seemed at the time to be an endless tunnel called seminary, with very little evidence to reassure us that our condition would change much at the other end of the tunnel. First-year seminary graduates are not known for the lucrative contracts they sign with churches of national renown. We just hoped we'd find a position in ministry that would put food on the table and pay our few bills.

START WHERE YOU ARE

The reason I have shared a little about our condition and prospects at the beginning of seminary is to help you understand what our mind-set and environment were when we sat down at that kitchen table to begin fleshing out some goals for our future. We had no reason to expect that anything unexpected or miraculous was going to happen to radically alter the course of our life. But we did have reason to expect that the God who had clearly led us to seminary had done so for a reason and that we should begin preparing ourselves for whatever opportunities he might present. With all of that in mind, we sat down to talk and write.

We began developing our goals using a grid similar to the one that follows:

	1 Year	5 Years	10+ Years
Spiritual			
Intellectual			
Physical			
Relational			
Professional			
Financial			

We looked at the different areas of our lives (spiritual, intellectual, physical, relational, professional, and financial) in terms of a one-year, five-year, and ten-year block of time. We then asked ourselves a very simple question, "Where would we like to be in each of these areas one, five, and ten years in the future?" We initially did this exercise for us as a couple, later we did it for ourselves individually.

When we were finished with our chart, a process that actually took more than one session, we posted it on our refrigerator. I can still remember seeing that avocado green sheet of paper on our banana yellow fridge countless times a day for several years. In all honesty, we never spent much time talking about those goals that we'd written and posted. We never had a strategy session to plan how we would make them happen. Both Sue and I just saw them and read quick snippets every time we opened the refrigerator or sat at the kitchen table.

AN AMAZING THING HAPPENED!

Looking back at our goal-setting exercise nearly twenty years later, both Sue and I have been amazed time and again by the incredible number of those original goals that have become reality. Inexplicably, most of those goals we set together back in 1982 have been realized.

Some of the goals we optimistically wrote down that first year of seminary were things like . . .

Become ministering members of a local church (spiritual; 1 year)

See some family members come to Christ (spiritual; 10+ years)

Complete our family (relational; 5–10 years)

Graduate from seminary (professional; 5 years)

Become a senior pastor (professional; 5–10 years)

Complete a doctoral degree (intellectual; 10+ years)

Maintain a healthy, happy, growing marriage (relational & spiritual; 1, 5, 10+ years)

Develop a "reading" family (relational & intellectual; 5–10 years)

Own a home (financial; 10+ years)

Write and have at least one book published (professional, intellectual & financial; 10+ years)

See all of our children come to Christ (spiritual; 10+ years)

These are just some of the goals we set together, each of them articulated in more detail for our purposes. Today every one of the goals I listed above has been realized! It is important to remember where we were professionally, financially, and so on when we wrote those goals. We had absolutely no reason at that time to believe that we would ever have the finances or the opportunity to begin, let alone complete, a doctoral program, but we did. The goal of writing a book was about as close to fantasy as I could get at the time. Yet the words I am writing are part of my second book, with several others in the works. Without any help from either of our families, we were able to purchase a brand-new home in 1987, just five years after our goal-setting exercise.

All four of our children have accepted Christ and are growing in their faith—and, yes, two of them are teenagers. Each of our children is a voracious reader and is reading beyond his or her age/grade level. Our youngest, Sammy Jr., is currently in the third grade and is reading at a sixth-grade level.

Now the reason I share these outcomes is not to impress you but to impress on you the almost mystical power of goals. I am convinced that God used our time of prayerfully considering our future to place us on the course he was preparing for us. None of these outcomes happened because we are exceptional or extraordinarily gifted people—our families and friends would be quick to dispel that notion. Clearly they are all the result of God's sheer mercy and grace. But beyond that, I am convinced they stand as a testament to the vision, power, and motivation that can be created by simply articulating and being regularly exposed to the specific goals that we set for our lives.

WHY SET GOALS?

There are many reasons for setting goals. Some reasons are for purely self-serving, materialistic, and self-aggrandizing purposes. We are told by many goal-setting gurus that the world is ours for the taking. If we will simply step up to the plate and take our well-orchestrated swings, we will eventually connect with the pitch and hit what for us will be a grand slam. Setting goals will help us get ahead in life, we're told. Goals can help us make our mark in the world. In fact some goal-setting advocates and the workshops they facilitate advocate something much closer to magical, mind-over-matter, speak-your-own-reality hocus-pocus than strategic, constructive goal setting that can bring life change. If you can envision what you want and focus on it for long enough, it will become reality, they say.

That was my initial exposure to goal setting when I was unceremoniously immersed in the world of goal-driven multilevel marketing. I was convinced by my multilevel marketing mentor that if I would listen to enough "dream building" tapes and plaster enough color pictures of the cars, boats, and houses I was yearning for all over my home, I would be "programmed" to achieve whatever I was able to believe.

However, that is not the type of goal setting I am promoting as a foundational aspect of self-leadership. Rather, I believe that setting goals is one of the primary ways we can direct our lives. I do not mean "direct" in the sense of acquiring short-term, materialistic objects of our affection. It's not like saving up to get that new car or house you've wanted. Nor do I use the term "direct" to in any way suggest that we are the ultimate sovereign of our life. The goal setting I am talking about is not even about setting your sights on some specific career position that you hope to achieve at some point in the future.

Instead, one of the primary purposes of setting what I will call Life Goals is to give our lives direction; direction that is consistent with what we have already articulated to be our life's values and Calling. Once we understand our life's values well enough to articulate them in written form and we understand what our true life's Calling is, then we can begin to utilize goal setting as a way to ensure that our life is constantly moving in the direction of our stated values and Calling.

Looking back on the goals that my wife and I set during our early years in seminary, we can see that not all of the goals we set are consistent with my present understanding of what I would now consider worthy life goals. There were some goals we set, such as owning our own home, that were purely personal and material in nature. That is not to say that such a goal should not be set. Rather, I am simply saying that is not the *type* of goal I am advocating in the context of self-leadership.

WHAT'S A LIFE GOAL?

In the simplest sense, a goal is a target, of sorts, that we set for ourselves. A goal is something for which we aim, a target that we haven't yet hit. We have not yet arrived at that place we have envisioned. Thus a goal represents a future state that is somehow different from our present state. As such, the space between our present state and the goal we have set, which represents a desired future state, is the ethereal, obstacle-strewn, no-man's-land through which we must skillfully and persistently navigate our life if we are going to reach our destination.

When we set a goal of any type, that goal presupposes that a journey of sorts must be undertaken. It is with this basic understanding of the concept of a goal that I would like to propose what will become our working definition.

For the purposes of self-leadership, a life goal is a planned conflict with the status quo that results in a lifelong journey. When we set a goal, we are strategically planning an assault on the status quo, or present state of our life, in an effort to move to a new, more desirable place.

In essence, the difference between a life goal and any other type of goal we may set has to do with the intention and reason that lies behind the goal. It is not that the wording or format of the goal is noticeably different. What makes a life goal different is the reason for setting it in the first place.

Using again what is likely the most universal of human goals, the goal to lose weight, let's think about what makes it a worthy life goal. If the goal of losing weight is primarily set so that we will look better at our twentieth high school reunion and impress our former classmates, it does not qualify as a life goal. If, however, we set the same goal—the goal to lose weight—but the primary intention driving this goal is to create a healthier physical body with which we can more effectively carry out our Calling and better manifest our values, it then becomes a worthy life goal.

Now you may think that this is nothing more than an exercise in creative semantics, but it is much more than that and produces profoundly different outcomes. Take, for example, the goal of losing weight we have just discussed. What happens in the first case when the reunion is over? What happens to the goal? When the lights go out and the band stops playing at the reunion, the goal has been achieved. The stated destination has been reached—the target has been hit. That is not necessarily bad, but it is, one must admit, rather shortsighted and superficial. There

85

is a very high likelihood, now that our classmates have been duly impressed, that the disciplines and practices that propelled us on our weight-loss journey will cease. Our purpose has been achieved. If we are to maintain the weight loss, we will need to develop another motivation for keeping the weight off.

When our goal to lose weight is driven by the desire to promote our long-term health—which will, in turn, enhance our ability to exercise our life's Calling and manifest our life values—the goal represents a destination that will require a journey of more than a few months and extends beyond reaching a desired weight. If we are successful, a goal of this nature will have a much greater impact on our life over the long term than will the goal to lose weight when driven by the desire to impress others.

Not S.M.A.R.T. Goals

What I am suggesting here is in direct opposition to much that you have previously been exposed to when it comes to the topic of setting successful goals.

Most of us have been schooled in the technique of setting what are called S.M.A.R.T. goals. This is an acronym that stands for goals that are: Specific, Measurable, Attainable, Realistic, and have a specific Time frame. This is a great tool for setting goals and one that I use regularly in setting certain goals. However, when it comes to goals that are worthy of propelling us on a lifelong journey of self-leadership and growth, S.M.A.R.T. goals alone are not sufficient.

The reality is that we need some goals in life that are not realistic from a human perspective. The apostle Paul seemed to articulate a life goal when he said in Philippians 3:12, "I don't mean to say that I have already achieved these things or that I have already reached perfection! But I keep working toward that day when I will finally be all that Christ Jesus saved me for and wants me to be." This was clearly a goal toward which Paul aspired. In fact it can be safely said that everything he did in his life was done with the purpose of making progress toward this lofty goal—a goal that obviously is not a typical S.M.A.R.T. goal.

However, I am convinced that it was only an expansive life goal of this magnitude that could have motivated Paul to endure great suffering and hardship and still achieve so much. His goal of taking the good news of the gospel to the ends of the known world was not, from a strictly human perspective, specific, realistic, or attainable. Similarly, Abraham's following the voice of God to a land in which he had never been, believing he would become a great nation, clearly would not qualify as a realistic goal. Neither was it specific or measurable, according to the S.M.A.R.T. goal paradigm. Joshua's goal of conquering the world's existing superpowers with a ragtag group of nomads who had virtually no military experience would not be considered realistic by most. And yet without doubt it was a worthy goal.

As we engage in the practice of self-leadership, we must not be reductionistic in our thinking when it comes to the goals or directions we desire to set for our life. It is vital that we see our life in an eternal perspective and recognize that our life is much too expansive to be directed adequately by simple, short-term goals alone. Though I am in no way suggesting that short-term S.M.A.R.T.–type goals have no place in effective self-leadership, I am suggesting that such goals must be seen as a very small piece of the goal-setting puzzle when it comes to effectively leading our life. I will speak more about short-term goals later.

SETTING LIFE GOALS

There are some helpful guidelines we can use when we are developing our life goals. These guidelines are a series of questions that we should ask of the goal or course of action we are proposing in an effort to help us identify whether or not it qualifies as a life goal according to our definition.

Question One: *Which of my specific values will this goal most effectively embody and enable me to better flesh out or manifest in my life?*

Question Two: *In what specific ways does this goal or course of action enable me to better live out my life's Calling?*

Question Three: *How does this goal enable me to more effectively contribute to the advancement of God's kingdom on earth?*

Question Four: *In what ways would my life's Calling be impeded and my values undermined or ignored if this goal were not set?*

Question Five: *Is this a goal that is worthy of Christ himself? Is this a goal that Jesus might have entertained during his earthly life?*

Question Six: *Will the pursuit of this goal facilitate my development in Christ-likeness and move me closer to becoming all God desires me to be (not do)?*

The intentions and motives that underlie our actions and behaviors are what give them purpose and meaning and can qualify them as worthy life goals.

SOME SAMPLE LIFE GOALS

So, then, what exactly does a life goal look like? Below I have listed just a few of my life goals in an effort to help you get a handle on what it is I have been talking about. Before you read these, it is important for you to realize that there is no specific formula that must be followed when writing a life goal. The only criteria is that the goal satisfy the six guidelines for life goals just given.

SAM'S LIFE GOALS

I will contribute to the continual growth and advancement of Christ's church on earth by maintaining involvement in the formation and equipping of spiritual leaders who are capable of multiplying my efforts.

I will devote quality time to my wife, Sue, in an effort to share my life with her and nurture her unique gifts, abilities, and interests.

I will treat every other person I relate with exactly as I would like to be treated and do all in my power, with God's help, to make them feel valued and loved as individuals of genuine worth.

I will maintain self-control of my eating habits and exercise five days a week in an effort to maintain a peak level of physical fitness for my age and the health necessary to live out my Calling in a way that brings God glory.

These goals flow directly from the values that I have articulated and are also consistent with my life Calling, as I have perceived it. Each of the goals I have just listed also passes muster according to the six guidelines for goal setting.

Noticeably missing from each of the life goals I have listed are most of the elements espoused for S.M.A.R.T. goals. These goals are too expansive to comfortably fit within such constraints. However, if these goals are ever going to be realized, it will require that each of them be accompanied by a series of short-term tactical steps. This is the appropriate place in the goal-setting process, then, at which we make use of techniques such as S.M.A.R.T. goals.

It is also important to note that life goals will not need to be changed from year to year. They represent the direction in which we have determined to lead our life to its end. As a result, we will not have to create new life goals repeatedly. It is true that we may add new life goals as we grow and mature and are better able to understand our Calling and the direction in which God is leading us, but these will likely be added to our existing life goals rather than replacing them.

In summary, we could say that worthy life goals are, in actuality, statements of intention and purpose that reflect the ultimate direction in which we are leading our life. They do not merely represent tasks and short-term outcomes, but rather lifelong aspirations without which our life would experience a lack of direction.

KINGDOM-SIZED GOALS

There is no doubt that one of the most amazing feats ever accomplished in the history of our nation was the epic journey of Meriwether Lewis and William Clark through the untamed wilderness that lay west of the Missouri River in 1803. In an attempt to chart an all-water course to the Pacific Ocean, Lewis and Clark were faced with a goal of monumental proportions—what one might well consider the goal of a lifetime.

During the years 1803–1806, the expedition led by these two explorers accomplished things that most people would be quick to deem impossible—even today. And yet, enduring all forms of hardship, suffering, and sacrifice, Lewis and Clark successfully navigated their way to the Pacific and back again, providing our adolescent nation with the discoveries and knowledge necessary to settle, cultivate, and reap the bounty of the limitless resource known as the Louisiana Purchase.

On their return, Lewis and Clark were hailed as international heroes, and rightly so. However, as daunting as the goal was and as rich the reward, it was simply not enough to satisfy the inner yearning of a man like Meriwether Lewis, whose inner landscape was more expansive than the wilderness he conquered. In 1809, just a few short years after the completion of his historic journey, with nothing left in his life he felt worthy of pursuing, Meriwether Lewis fell frequently into depression and despondency. Though he often struggled throughout his life with what was at that time called melancholy, his frequent adventures and energetic goals kept the beast of boredom and depression at bay most of his life. But after the great expedition, with no other new lands to chart, or so he thought, Lewis began drinking heavily and taking powerful drugs in an effort to deal with his despondency. Finally, on October 11, 1809, the great explorer, who felt there was nothing left to do with his life, committed suicide at a remote country inn along the Natchez Trace Trail in what today is Tennessee.

For Meriwether Lewis, one enormous life goal was simply too small for his life. He could not think beyond that Herculean accomplishment to anything more meaningful in which he could invest his life, so he tragically ended it.

As Christian leaders we must be careful that we not set goals that are too small for our God and the Calling he has issued us. Goals that are truly worthy of our life are kingdom-sized goals that will never be completely achieved during this lifetime. We need to take the time and effort needed to set goals that will require the very best we have to offer over the course of our lifetime. Life goals are God-sized goals.

A SELF-LEADERSHIP WORKSHOP

Following is a series of exercises that will guide you through the process of synthesizing your values and Calling into some worthy life goals. At the completion of this exercise it is hoped that you will have created for yourself a document that has the potential to effectively guide you in your efforts to exercise meaningful self-leadership, which, in turn, will greatly maximize the investment of your life for the glory of God.

After once again reviewing your life values, as well as your ideal avocation as articulated in the workshop section of chapter 3, take some time to write some life goals for yourself. Write your life goals using the six guidelines on pages 87–88. Write them in the grid on page 92.

Before you begin, consider the following thought-prompting questions. They may unearth goals that you haven't yet verbalized but that need to be included in your life goals.

Are there any life values you feel you need to be more dedicated to effectively living out?

Are there any ways you would like to fulfill your Calling more consistently and effectively?

Are there any directions in which you should be moving or any actions you should be taking in an effort to identify and engage in a new avocation that would serve as a better platform for you?

After writing down your life goals, take some time to loosely rank them in the order of their importance to living out your values and Calling. One method that you can use to determine the priority of your life goals is to begin with the first one you list and compare it to the next one on the list. Take some time to

91

reflect on both of them and decide which of the two is more important to living out your values and Calling. If you could only realize one of the two goals, which would best advance your values and Calling? Once you have made your decision, place a check beside the one that is less important and move on to compare the result with the next goal you have listed, following the same process of elimination for the entire list. The goal that survives through the first round of comparison is the most important life goal for you in light of your previously stated values and Calling. Then proceed to employ the same procedure until you have given a priority to each of your life goals.

Rank	Life Goals

5

MEASURING
YOUR LIFE'S MOTIVATION

Once you have articulated and embraced your life's values and after you have connected to some degree with your life's Calling and created some goals worthy of directing your life, you then must honestly measure your level of personal motivation to actually engage in the self-leadership necessary to effectively live out those values and realize your goals in the form of a called life. Simply identifying your values and understanding your Calling is not sufficient to realize your full leadership potential for God's glory—it takes something more.

THAT SOMETHING MORE

Mark Wellman knows how to climb mountains. In fact he is quite an accomplished climber with numerous difficult ascents to his credit. He is knowledgeable in the area of equipment and technique. Having extensive understanding of the physical fitness required for the rigors of climbing, he knows how to train his body for such endeavors. The truth is there are few climbers who have more knowledge and understanding than Mark Wellman when it comes to the skill of rock or mountain climbing. Mark's biggest challenge, however, is the fact that he is a paraplegic. His legs do not work at all from the hips down—what some would consider a serious obstacle when it comes to risking your life on a treacherous rock climb.

You see, all of the knowledge and expertise in the world is not going to get Mark up any mountain or on top of any major rock formation. For Mark, successful rock climbing requires a little something extra. And yet, in the summer of 1991, Mark became the first paraplegic to successfully climb the sheer rock face of the world-famous 2,200-foot-tall Half Dome rock formation in Yosemite National Park, a feat that is challenging enough for even the most physically fit, able-bodied climbers.

Though Mark's knowledge is essential, it does not give him the power to climb. Mustering the gumption to undertake such daunting challenges and complete successful climbs requires an extreme measure of personal motivation. Without the motivation, all of Mark's knowledge would leave him sitting at the bottom of Yosemite Valley in the shadow of the famous rock formation, wondering if a paraplegic could make such an ascent. For Mark Wellman, motivation is that something more that enables him to do what others only dream of.

KNOWLEDGE IS *NOT* POWER

It has been said by many that knowledge is power. The premise of this affirmation is that those individuals who monopolize the greatest amount of information and knowledge will be the most powerful people. In other words, a person's acquisition of knowledge and information will result in a corresponding degree of personal power and influence.

However, the reality is: Knowledge that is not applied is not power at all. In fact the exact opposite is true. The more information and knowledge a person possesses and yet refuses or fails to act on, for whatever reason, the more indicative it is of weakness and impotence than it is of power. Knowing what to do and doing what we know are two drastically different issues as we are all aware. Boldly acting on what we know to be true and applying the knowledge we possess to the issues of life can be thwarted on many different levels. Procrastination, fear, deception, lack of motivation, as well as desires for comfort and ease, among numerous other influences, can all conspire against us in such a way as to prevent the consistent application of what we know to the leading and living of our life.

Today as never before the American public possesses abundant information on the dangers and health risks of smoking. In addition, virtually everyone's knowledge concerning the risks of smoking has been reinforced by some painful personal experience as they have watched a relative or friend suffer the ill effects of this destructive habit. And yet there does not seem to be a direct correlation between our increased knowledge of the dangers of smoking and the power to quit the habit. Additionally, our plethora of information in this area is not enough to prevent new smokers from taking up the habit every day. In this particular case, I am sure most would agree, knowledge alone is not power.

Similarly, we have all witnessed the reality that information and knowledge alone do not confer the power or ability to practically apply that knowledge even when it is possessed by a leader of great intellect and influence.

When President Clinton engaged in his reckless affair with White House intern Monica Lewinsky during the years 1995 through 1997, he possessed information that should have prevented such moronic behavior. The president was well aware of the fact that there was an independent prosecutor investigating possible wrongdoing in which he may have been involved. Mr. Clinton knew Paula Corbin Jones was suing him for sexual harassment and that discovery in the case was ongoing. Furthermore, the president also had knowledge that his political adversaries were mounting a campaign to undermine his presidency. And yet, in spite of all this knowledge and information, the president still was not able to translate his knowledge into practice.

Consequently, his failure to apply what he knew has been extremely costly for him, his family, his friends, and our country.

But before we too quickly pass judgment on our apparently hapless president or condemn those we consider ignorant for continuing to smoke in the face of overwhelmingly negative information, we must all admit that we suffer from the same malady to one degree or another. All too often we know what we should do; we possess all of the necessary information, and yet we still fail to allow our knowledge to produce the corresponding action. Whether it's a failure to lose weight when we know that we should, our resistance to a low-fat diet when we know that our cholesterol is out of control, or our refusal to exercise when we know that it will greatly benefit our health and possibly extend our life, we all know how difficult it can be to make that difficult transition from information to application.

MOTIVATION—THE MISSING LINK

When it comes to the exercise of effective self-leadership, knowledge alone is not enough. Something more is required that will enable us to make the critical transition from information to application. That something more is the illusive concept we know as motivation. For many leaders and would-be leaders, motivation is the missing link when it comes to the effective exercise of self-leadership. It is our level of motivation, or its absence, that will determine how effectively and how consistently we apply what we know to the leading of our life.

As we begin self-discipline for more effective self-leadership, it is important that we understand the role our motivation plays in the process. Undoubtedly we have all jokingly said at one time or another, "The spirit is willing but the flesh is weak," as we tried to rationalize our failure to do something we should have done or justify something we did that we shouldn't have. Regardless of how lightheartedly we may have quoted this Scripture in the past, it does accurately represent the crux of effective self-leadership. It speaks to the issue and importance of motivation.

As laudatory as it may be for us to identify and clearly articulate our life's values and connect with our life's true Calling, neither of these activities will bear much fruit if we are not able to orchestrate our daily activities so that they are consistent with our values and facilitate our Calling. The often missing link between our values and Calling and our effective self-leadership is our level of motivation. How motivated are we to make the changes that must be made in our life to ensure that we are living a truly value-driven life that flows out of a deep sense of Calling? It is a crucial question but one that we seldom take the time to ask, let alone answer.

So what exactly is motivation and how do we go about measuring it? Motivation is one of those concepts that can be somewhat like Jell-O—as soon as you think you have it on your definitional spoon, it falls off again. Simply stated, motivation involves "an internal state of being that impels or drives us to action. . . . Motivation is an energizer of behavior."[1]

While it may seem simple enough to define motivation, the plot thickens when we attempt to describe and understand the "how" of motivation. What is it that actually causes us to be internally impelled or driven to take certain actions and abstain from others? When it comes to the "how" of motivation, there are several mechanisms at work that we must consider: our basic needs, psychological drives, willful desires, and significant beliefs.

BASIC NEEDS

The first mechanism at work within us that can impel or drive us to take action in a given area has to do with our basic needs as human beings. One of our most basic needs is our need for air to breathe. We simply must have it or we will die. As a result, when we are deprived of oxygen for some reason, that basic need will compel us to take action in an effort to get oxygen. In fact we will be compelled, or highly motivated, to do whatever is necessary until our need is satisfied. Conversely, when we are breathing easily and our body's need for oxygen is being adequately met, we will not be motivated to search for oxygen. A satisfied need is not a motivator.

In the spring of 1987, a week before Easter Sunday, I awoke one night unable to breathe. My chest felt as if it were being compressed by a five-hundred-pound weight. As I sprang from bed that night, the only thing on my mind was getting the air I needed into my lungs. I gasped and wheezed and sucked in an effort to get the oxygen I needed but was unsuccessful. So I rushed to the bathroom, ran some scalding hot water into the sink, and with a heavy towel over my head, stuck my face close to the steaming water. It didn't help me to breathe any easier. Finally, I woke up my wife and she rushed me to the emergency room in Anaheim Hills, California, where the doctors worked for more than eight hours to stabilize my breathing. Once the acute emergency was over, it was determined that I had a serious viral lung infection that had inflamed my airways and prevented my breathing.

During those frightening hours when I was struggling to breathe, I really was not thinking of much else. I didn't feel motivated to do anything but get air! I wasn't motivated to eat. I wasn't motivated to shower or look good. I didn't feel driven to impress anyone. All I cared about was satisfying my need for oxygen.

You see, one of the ways that we can measure our level of motivation in a certain area of our life is to determine our current level of need. If, for example, you are trying to motivate yourself to lose weight, how desperately do you feel the need to do so? Remember that a satisfied need is not a motivator. So if you are trying to motivate yourself to take the actions necessary to lose five pounds, on the basis of need, it probably will be a pretty tough sell. The need to lose five pounds probably isn't acute enough to motivate much action. On the other hand, if your physician tells you that you need to lose forty pounds or you may die, the need factor goes way up and it is easier to find the motivation to take the appropriate actions. Thus, as we have seen, basic needs can be powerful mechanisms that create within us a motivation to act.

For our purposes in determining our motivation to achieve a goal, we consider not only our most basic physical needs, such as food and water, but also our needs for basic physical safety. In addition, any acute needs that we may currently be experiencing

98

and that seem to be constantly occupying our thoughts should be considered here as well. For example, a troubled relationship with a significant person in our life or a pressing need for employment should be considered basic needs. A personal financial crisis or a serious physical illness would also be the types of issues in our life that we should consider basic needs.

PHYSIOLOGICAL DRIVES

Another source of motivation comes in the form of neurological and biochemical drives. These primary physiological drives, as they are sometimes called, include such things as sleep, avoidance of pain, the experience of pleasure, and sex, among other drives. Again, when these drives are at issue, we will be highly motivated to take action in an effort to satisfy them. When we begin to feel sleepy, we become motivated to search out a place to sleep. The stronger the urge to sleep becomes, the more active we will be in our efforts to satisfy our need for sleep. However, once we have enjoyed a refreshing sleep, we will not be highly motivated to sleep again until such time as our body signals its renewed need for sleep.

Other drives that can be highly motivating are our drives to avoid pain and to experience pleasure. We are highly motivated to avoid painful experiences in life, whether the pain is physical or emotional. That is one of the reasons many people are not highly motivated to engage in regular exercise, because they associate it with both physical and emotional pain. On some level most people want to exercise but they are not sufficiently motivated to take action because for them exercise means the pain of exhaustion and sore muscles rather than the pleasure of good health, a fit body, and renewed energy. Thus their drive to avoid pain serves as a motivation to not take action.

Our physiological drives are any drives that are essential to the comfortable and healthy maintenance of our physical and emotional existence. When we begin to assess our readiness to take action in a certain area, we should measure the level of motivation that will be provided by our physiological drives.

Willful Desires

When we consider desires as a mechanism that can create a motivation to act, we move into the realm of the mind and the exercise of human will in contrast to basic human needs or physiological drives. Our desires are not so much a function of our physiology as they are a function of our will. When most of our basic needs have been met and our drives satisfied, we then begin to contemplate other things that we want or activities in which we would like to engage.

We may desire success, a sense of personal worth, the acquisition of material possessions, education, social status, power, spiritual meaning, a transcendent purpose for our being, feelings of forgiveness and countless other feelings, objects, and activities. Though our desires are not regulated by our physiology as are our basic human needs and our drives for things such as food, water, and sleep, they are, nonetheless, extremely potent as motivators and worthy of our careful reflection as we determine what motivates us.

Eighteenth-century theologian and revivalist Jonathan Edwards wrote in his classic work *Freedom and Will* that human will and desire are "not so entirely distinct that they can ever be properly said to run counter. A man never, in any instance, wills anything contrary to his desires, or desires anything contrary to his will."[2] In other words, according to Edwards, we as human beings always act according to our desires. Furthermore, the determining element in whether or not a particular desire will create within us a compelling bias for action involves how strong that desire is at any given moment. If we have a relatively low desire to do something or to have something, it is unlikely that we will be spurred to action.

The reality is that at any given point in time we have many different desires, but generally it is our most acute desire that will motivate us to take action. Measuring our motivation to live out our values in the form of a called life will by necessity require that we honestly assess the intensity of our desires.

Significant Beliefs

A final mechanism that we must take into consideration when measuring our motivation to take action has to do with our beliefs. The deeply held beliefs of human beings can actually supersede and hold sway over all of the previously mentioned motivational mechanisms.

If a belief is strong enough, it can motivate us to take action that is actually contrary at some levels to our basic human needs, physiological drives, and willful desires. Our beliefs, coupled with an intense desire to live and act consistently with our beliefs, can create without question one of the strongest motivators toward action. That is why the process of identifying and articulating our life's values or beliefs is so foundational to the effective exercise of self-leadership.

Our drive to satisfy our physical hunger—I am sure most people would agree—is a powerful motivator to action. However, if we were placed in circumstances where we were forced to choose between satisfying our own hunger or the hunger of our child, our deeply held belief that we are responsible for our child's well-being as well as our strong desire to see our child cared for and protected, would very likely motivate us to neglect our own needs in favor of meeting our child's need.

There have been countless martyrs down through history who have willingly endured excruciating physical pain and suffering and given up their lives, motivated by a deeply held belief that overcame their natural drive toward physical preservation.

Generations of Americans have willingly chosen to endure hunger, thirst, deprivation of sleep, and extreme discomfort for prolonged periods of time, during numerous wars and conflicts, all because of their deep belief in personal freedom and the principles of a democratic republic.

Beliefs in propositions and principles such as truth, freedom, God, fairness, eternal life, sanctity of life, forgiveness, sacrifice, and many others can be strong motivators. Bear in mind that our beliefs are distinct from our desires in that they are based in metaphysical realities that remain constant whether we happen to be aware of those realities or not. Our desires, however, change depending on our circumstances.

Our level of motivation to take action when it comes to any activity, goal, or decision will always be a composite of these four mechanisms—basic needs, physiological drives, willful desires, and significant beliefs—at work in our life at any given time. But exactly how can we determine our level of motivation when we are contemplating a new goal or course of action in life? Is there any way that we can quantify these four mechanisms in a way that will help us determine the likelihood of success before we begin?

DETERMINING OUR MOTIVATION FACTOR

Admittedly, any attempts to quantify something as illusive as motivation is a subjective proposition. At the same time, anything we can do to help determine how motivated we are to take action in a certain area will be helpful. Albeit a crude tool, I have developed the Motivational Factor Grid (MFG) as a means of quantifying what our motivation factor (MF) is in any given situation. Our motivation factor, in turn, can help us measure the degree to which the necessary bias for action will be created in that situation.

The MFG can be used to help determine our potential for success in any course of action by identifying our motivation factor for the specific action being contemplated. Of course, the MFG will only be accurate and helpful to the degree that we understand the dynamics of each of the four motivating mechanisms (MM) and are able to provide an honest assessment of the degree to which they are operational in our life at any given time.

To use the MFG, simply write the action being contemplated in the space to the right of the heading "Goal or Desired Action." Then, for each MM listed in the left-hand column, determine the degree to which that MM is a factor in the goal or action you are evaluating by placing the number (1 through 5) in the score box at the right-hand side of the grid. When finished, total all scores to arrive at your MF, which should be no lower than 4 and no higher than 20. Then, using your MF, find the likelihood that it will create the necessary bias for action on the scale at the bottom of the grid. Obviously, the higher your MF, the greater the potential for success when undertaking the contemplated task.

Motivational Factor Grid

Goal or Desired Action:						
Motivating Mechanism	Degree mechanism is a factor in contemplated action					Score
	Not at all	Some-what	Moder-ately	Strongly	Intensely	
Basic Needs	1	2	3	4	5	
Physiological Drives	1	2	3	4	5	
Willful Desires	1	2	3	4	5	
Significant Beliefs	1	2	3	4	5	

Motivational Factor (MF)

Likelihood MF will create bias toward action		
4	5–11	12–20
Low	Moderate	High

Before using the MFG it will be helpful to review the motivational mechanisms on pages 97–102.

MEASURING THE MOTIVATION OF MOSES

Let's consider the life of Moses again as an example. Utilizing the Motivational Factor Grid we can determine how motivated Moses may have been to respond to God's call to liberate the people from Egypt. Based on what we know about the life of Moses from the biblical record, did he have a motivation factor that could reasonably be expected to produce the necessary bias for action? Let's briefly examine the motivational mechanisms and how they may have come into play in Moses' situation.

Based on what we know about Moses and his previous experiences in Egypt, he would probably score a 2 in the area of basic needs. We can consider as a basic need Moses' need to resolve the emotionally painful and unsettled episode that caused him to flee Egypt as a wanted felon. No doubt there was some aspect of God's invitation that appealed to Moses because it would resolve and bring to some emotional closure this traumatic and life-shaping episode from his past.

In addition, I am convinced it could be argued that Moses still felt a deep need to see his people liberated from their cruel slavery. Though these issues were probably present at the time Moses received this challenge, it is doubtful that they would have been intensely at work in this situation. As a result, I have given Moses a 2 for this motivational mechanism, recognizing that the area of basic needs, as we have described it, was only somewhat a factor in this decision he had to make.

In the area of physiological needs, Moses probably would have been highly motivated *not* to take action because doing so would likely result in increased physical discomfort and pain and possibly loss of life. With this in mind there was not much reason for Moses to be motivated to go to Egypt and more reason to stay in Midian. So I give Moses a 1 for this motivational mechanism.

Physiological Drives	1

When we come to the area of willful desires, we are getting closer to the motivational mechanism that could produce the necessary bias to take action. One could argue that Moses had a desire to be successful in light of his earlier failure—he wanted to make a difference. Such a mission could provide Moses with a sense of purpose and Calling. Going to Egypt to be God's instrument of liberation, if successful, could result in a measure of renewed self-worth. Accepting that such a mission might also add to Moses' personal sense of spiritual meaning—knowing that he was being used by God to liberate God's chosen people—it is reasonable to assume that Moses' desire had a very strong influence on him. Thus I give him a 5 for this motivational mechanism.

Willful Desires	5

The mechanism of significant beliefs would likely provide Moses with the greatest bias toward action in making this decision. His deeply held beliefs about God, God's chosen people, the importance of obedience, God's ability to provide for the mission, his belief that the people were wrongly enslaved, and many other significant beliefs would give Moses a score of 5 for this mechanism.

Significant Beliefs	5

This would give Moses a Motivation Factor of 13, which, according to our scale, would likely produce a high bias toward action. And, as we know, Moses did take action and was successful in his efforts.

It's interesting to note that if we were to apply the same evaluation to the motivational mechanisms at work in Pharaoh's life, when initially faced with the decision to let the people go, it might look something like this: basic needs—1; physiological drives—1; willful desires—1; and significant beliefs—1. This would give Pharaoh a motivation factor of 4, which would produce a very low bias toward action, which was, in fact, consistent with his initial actions. It was only as the motivational mechanisms of basic needs and physiological drives increased as a

105

result of the manifestation of the plagues that Pharaoh was ultimately motivated to let the people go.

Though the Motivational Factor Grid is in no way a scientific or foolproof tool, it does provide us with a somewhat objective way to measure our level of motivation when considering whether or not to launch out on some grand venture or undertake a new course of action in our life.

WHEN MOTIVATION IS MISSING

What can you do when you are faced with a course of action that you really should take and yet you don't seem to have the motivation that will result in your taking action? Is there a way that you can elevate your low motivation factor and thus increase the likelihood of success? Let me suggest at least two potential exercises that may have the effect of increasing your motivation to act. These exercises will increase your MF by helping you see more clearly, or maybe in an entirely new way, how the considered action actually interfaces with your basic needs, physiological drives, willful desires, or significant beliefs.

WHAT IF . . . ?

The first exercise that can help you increase your level of motivation when faced with a certain task or when considering a new course of action involves asking yourself the question, What if . . . ? What if I fail to take this action?

Once this question has been asked, it is important to devote some concentrated thought to providing a realistic answer to the question. As you do, be careful not to overdramatize and, at the same time, don't fall victim to the all-too-human tendency to minimize the consequences that are likely should you opt not to take the action under consideration.

For example, if you are considering engaging in a weight-loss program but are struggling with the motivation to do so, take a piece of paper and at the top of the page write the question, What if I fail to take any action to lose weight? Consider what will be the probable results if you choose to maintain the status quo in this area. Then begin to list the results you will experience during the course of the next year or two if nothing at all changes in this area of your life. Your list might look something like this:

What if I fail to take any action to lose weight?

If I fail to take the action necessary to lose weight I can expect to experience:

1. poor health
2. low self-esteem
3. being a poor example to my family and those I lead
4. feeling terrible both emotionally and physically
5. increasing obesity—I will continue to gain weight if nothing changes
6. increased weight, making it more difficult to lose weight in the future
7. unhappiness with my appearance
8. not being able to wear the clothes I like
9. fewer options in life in terms of activities in which I can participate
10. feeling self-conscious when I speak publicly
11. less influence as a leader
12. a shorter life—added weight decreases life-expectancy
13. increasing folds of unsightly flab on my body!

I have chosen this as an example because I am sure it is one with which most of us can identify. However, we need to engage in the same exercise for any of the areas in which we are struggling with a low motivation factor. One of the reasons that we are often not motivated to take a necessary action is because we have never really taken the time to consider what will happen if we fail to take that action. Remember that one of our primary physiological drives is to avoid pain. If we can help ourselves see the painful reality of failing to take the necessary action, it can have the effect of increasing our motivation level.

You may ask, "Why focus on the negative? Why not focus instead on the positive benefits of losing weight? Wouldn't that be a more powerful motivation?" For some individuals I suppose it may be. But it is more likely that by focusing on the future state we hope to achieve, we become discouraged and hopeless because our goal seems so out of reach. By posting pictures of a perfect body on the fridge or your bathroom mirror, not only do you begin to focus on the purely physical and aesthetic aspects of the change you desire, you are also creating for yourself a possibly unachievable goal. Many, then, give up their efforts out of frustration. Human beings are much more motivated to avoid pain than to gain pleasure, and it is often more effective to review several times a day all of the pain you will create for yourself if you fail to consistently take action in this area of your life.

The same exercise could be employed to help increase your motivation to better manage your personal finances, improve a struggling marriage, continue your education, take a new risk, change careers or jobs, step into new areas of leadership, devote more time to your family, begin the regular practice of spiritual disciplines, or even something like adding regular times of recreation into your hectic schedule.

Regardless of the area with which you find yourself struggling with low motivation, you can likely increase your motivation by seriously engaging in this exercise.

THE ROCKING CHAIR TEST

The second exercise is quite simple and yet can be rather profound. If you find yourself struggling to take action in a particular area, take the Rocking Chair Test. Imagine yourself at eighty or ninety years old, clearly toward the sunset of your active life, and consider how you would feel if you never engaged in the action for which you are struggling to find motivation.

How would you feel at the end of your life if you looked back and recognized that you simply refused to even attempt the effort to repair a damaged marriage or to write the book you often thought of writing or to exercise leadership in a new area. What will be the result at the end of your life to know you wasted years in ill health because you failed to take care of your body? What is it going to be like to experience being financially dependent on the state or loved ones because you failed to take the action required to manage your personal finances? These are some of the questions that we must answer if we want to avoid the painful results of refusing to take action in these important life areas.

One of the absolutely vital requirements for exercising effective self-leadership is to find the motivation necessary that will lead us to take action in the critical areas of our life. Simply knowing what is right or what we should do is not enough. The quality that sets effective leaders apart from others is that they are somehow able to muster the motivation required to make the positive changes and take the risks that others only longingly dream about. When it comes to self-leadership we must understand that knowledge is not power. Action is power. *The Scripture clearly states that when we know the right thing to do and fail or refuse to do it, for us it is sin* (see James 4:17). The most effective leaders have always known how to motivate themselves to action.

MOTIVATION TO SURVIVE A MOUNTAIN

In May of 1996 Dallas pathologist Beck Weathers attempted to do what few people have accomplished—scale the world's tallest mountain. Beck Weathers was on a team led by world-class mountaineer Scott Fischer, who was trying to successfully challenge the mystique and danger of Mount Everest. The attempt ended in the deaths of ten people, including two of the world's most well-known and experienced climbers—one of which was Scott Fischer.

The number of dead might have been eleven had it not been for the incredible survival of Beck Weathers against all odds. On that day in May, when the mountain claimed the lives of ten others, it made an effort at taking Beck's life as well.

109

Separated from the other members of his team as the result of snow blindness that was precipitated by an earlier eye surgery, Beck became lost in a blinding snow storm at 27,000 feet—an altitude known as the "death zone" by seasoned climbers. It was pitch black save for the faint glimmer of the moon working hard to seep through the small breaks in the storm clouds. The winds were in excess of 100 miles per hour, causing the temperature to plummet to 170 degrees below zero. Beck Weathers was lost on the side of the mountain with little or no vision and no supplies that would protect him against the fierce winds and cold. He stumbled along in a desperate search for the safety of camp, finally coming across several other stranded climbers. During his ordeal he lost one of his gloves and became so frostbitten and weary that he lay down in the snow with the others.

By the time the huddled group of frozen climbers were reached by a rescue effort, one of them had already frozen to death. As they checked Beck's vital signs, they realized that he was near death and any efforts to save him were hopeless. The arm of his gloveless hand was frozen solid at a 90 degree angle from his body and his naked hand was black with frostbite. He was barely breathing and clearly very near death. But Beck still had some life in him. Though every part of his body told him to give up, there was still a part of him that knew he had to take action if he was to survive. As he lay nearly submerged in what was rapidly becoming his snowy tomb, portions of his body literally frozen solid, Beck began to muster the motivation to take action. He began to run through his mind the faces of his children and his wife. He gazed into the future to his daughter's wedding and what it would be like for her to stand at the altar with no father to give her away. He thought of the grandchildren he would never hold and who would never know him. He considered his wife and what she would do without him during the coming years. And as Beck Weathers continued to contemplate the results of failing to take action, albeit action that most would have considered clearly impossible, he somehow got himself up out of the snowbank. As he gained his balance he simply began to walk, like an Egyptian mummy, arms extended, in the direction he hoped was where his team's high camp tents were pitched. Eventually he stumbled into the camp, and his amazed team members began the desperate attempts to save the frozen body of Beck Weathers. They carried him down the side of the mountain in an exhaustive and dangerous attempt to get him to an altitude where he might be rescued by helicopter.

Back in Dallas, Beck's wife, Peaches, had already been informed of Beck's death.

Finally, after what seemed like an eternity, Beck was lifted off of Everest by a heroic helicopter pilot who, by doing so, successfully completed the highest altitude rescue on record. Beck's life had been saved, but portions of his arms, nose, toes, and hands could not be salvaged.

Today Beck Weathers lives with a body that serves as a constant reminder not only of the dangers of Everest, but more important, the power of motivation. Every day that he sees his partial hands and looks in a mirror that reflects back a distorted, foreign image, he is reminded that he is capable of mustering the motivation to take action to achieve even what seems impossible.

My hope is that it will not take the menacing dangers of a Himalayan mountain to create the motivation we need to lead our lives effectively to the glory of God.

A SELF-LEADERSHIP WORKSHOP

Following is a series of activities and exercises that will help you measure your current level of motivation to live out the values and Calling you have already articulated. Then, based on what you discover, there is also space provided to engage in the What if . . . ? and Rocking Chair exercises in an effort to increase your level of motivation in any area if necessary.

1. Using the Motivational Factor Grids provided on page 112, list your life goals and rate your motivation for each of them. Review pages 102–3 if necessary.

2. Now list your life goals, in the order of importance determined in chapter 4. Write them in the grid at the bottom of page 114, then

write in the MF for each one and determine whether you have low, moderate, or high motivation to accomplish your goal (an MF of 4 or under is low; 5–11 is moderate; and 12–20 is high).

Goal or Desired Action:					
Motivating Mechanism	Degree mechanism is a factor in contemplated action				
	Not at all	Some-what	Moder-ately	Strongly	Intensely	Score
Basic Needs	1	2	3	4	5	
Physiological Drives	1	2	3	4	5	
Willful Desires	1	2	3	4	5	
Significant Beliefs	1	2	3	4	5	

Motivational Factor (MF)

Goal or Desired Action:					
Motivating Mechanism	Degree mechanism is a factor in contemplated action				
	Not at all	Some-what	Moder-ately	Strongly	Intensely	Score
Basic Needs	1	2	3	4	5	
Physiological Drives	1	2	3	4	5	
Willful Desires	1	2	3	4	5	
Significant Beliefs	1	2	3	4	5	

Motivational Factor (MF)

Goal or Desired Action:					
Motivating Mechanism	*Degree mechanism is a factor in contemplated action*				
	Not at all	Some-what	Moder-ately	Strongly	Intensely	Score
Basic Needs	1	2	3	4	5	
Physiological Drives	1	2	3	4	5	
Willful Desires	1	2	3	4	5	
Significant Beliefs	1	2	3	4	5	

Motivational Factor (MF)

Goal or Desired Action:					
Motivating Mechanism	*Degree mechanism is a factor in contemplated action*				
	Not at all	Some-what	Moder-ately	Strongly	Intensely	Score
Basic Needs	1	2	3	4	5	
Physiological Drives	1	2	3	4	5	
Willful Desires	1	2	3	4	5	
Significant Beliefs	1	2	3	4	5	

Motivational Factor (MF)

113

Goal or Desired Action:					
Motivating Mechanism	*Degree mechanism is a factor in contemplated action*				
	Not at all	Some-what	Moder-ately	Strongly	Intensely	Score
Basic Needs	1	2	3	4	5	
Physiological Drives	1	2	3	4	5	
Willful Desires	1	2	3	4	5	
Significant Beliefs	1	2	3	4	5	

Motivational Factor (MF)

Life Goals	Motivation Factor (1–20)	Bias for Action (Circle one)		
Goal 1:		Low	Moderate	High
Goal 2:		Low	Moderate	High
Goal 3:		Low	Moderate	High
Goal 4:		Low	Moderate	High
Goal 5:		Low	Moderate	High
Goal 6:		Low	Moderate	High
Goal 7:		Low	Moderate	High

3. For any of your goals with a bias for action below 8, complete either the What if . . . ?" exercise or the Rocking Chair Test in an effort to increase your current level of motivation.

Life Goal	What If . . . ? What if I fail to accomplish this goal?	Rocking Chair Test How will I feel near the end of my life if I don't attempt to accomplish this goal?

Life Goal	What If . . . ? What if I fail to accomplish this goal?	Rocking Chair Test How will I feel near the end of my life if I don't attempt to accomplish this goal?

Life Goal	What If . . . ?	Rocking Chair Test
	What if I fail to accomplish this goal?	How will I feel near the end of my life if I don't attempt to accomplish this goal?

Life Goal	What If . . . ?	Rocking Chair Test
	What if I fail to accomplish this goal?	How will I feel near the end of my life if I don't attempt to accomplish this goal?

Life Goal	What If . . . ?	Rocking Chair Test
	What if I fail to accomplish this goal?	How will I feel near the end of my life if I don't attempt to accomplish this goal?

4. For each life goal with a bias for action of 9 or above, list two actions you can take in the next three months to begin moving in the direction of the goal. See the example below.

Life Goal	Action
Life Goal #4: Stay physically fit	1. I will get up by 6 A.M. to allow for at least 45 minutes of physical fitness 5 days a week. 2. I will reduce the amount of calories consumed each day and steer clear of those foods that tempt me most.

Life Goal	Action

Life Goal	Action

Life Goal	Action

Life Goal	Action

117

Life Goal	Action

Life Goal	Action

Personal Constitution

Now, based on the work you've done so far, take time to create your personal statement of governing values and constitution. First, examples of the parts of a personal constitution are given to aid you in the process.

My Life's Calling
My life's Calling is to constantly strive, by the grace and power of God, to fully become all that God has created and saved me for (Phil. 3:12–14). I will do everything I can to maximize the gifts I have been graciously given in an effort to expand God's kingdom by accomplishing all the good things God prepared in advance of my life for me to do (Eph. 2:10).

119

My Basic Values	
God	*Governing Value Statement* I maintain a growing and increasingly intimate ~~conversational relationship with God.~~ *Definition* The single most vital and important value I hold is a personal belief in a living, loving, personal sovereign God. This God desires to interact with me. I will be conscious of my relationship with God and place it above every other value, priority, or goal. I will avoid every influence and activity that undermines my relationship with God.
Family	*Governing Value Statement* I love my wife as Christ loves the Church. *Definition* I will spend quality time with Sue to share my life with her and nurture her gifts, abilities, and interests. I desire to see her be the most effective, fulfilled, and productive person she can possibly be. I will consider her interests above my own.
Personal Health	*Governing Value Statement* I maintain my physical health, fitness, and appearance. *Definition* My body is the temple of the Holy Spirit of the living God and my only vehicle for accomplishing all that God desires me to accomplish. Thus I will maintain self-control in my eating habits. I will exercise my body at least five times a week and keep my weight under 180 pounds at all times. I will always give special attention to my personal appearance and look the best I possibly can.

My Life Goals
• I will contribute to the continual growth and advancement of Christ's church on earth by maintaining involvement in the formation and equipping of spiritual leaders who are capable of multiplying my efforts.
• I will devote quality time to my wife, Sue, in an effort to share my life with her and nurture her unique gifts, abilities, and interests.
• I will treat every person exactly as I would like to be treated and do all in my power, with God's help, to make each one feel valued and loved as an individual of genuine worth.
• I will maintain self-control of my eating habits and exercise five days a week in an effort to maintain a peak level of physical fitness for my age and the health necessary to live out my Calling in a way that brings God glory.

Space is given below for you to develop your own Personal Constitution. From chapter 3, insert your calling.
My Life's Calling:

List below your values and their definitions, as you wrote them in chapter 2. Add a governing value statement for each one.

121

My Basic Values	
	Governing Value Statement
	Definition
	Governing Value Statement
	Definition
	Governing Value Statement
	Definition
	Governing Value Statement
	Definition
	Governing Value Statement
	Definition

Continued

My Basic Values	
	Governing Value Statement
	Definition
	Governing Value Statement
	Definition
	Governing Value Statement
	Definition
	Governing Value Statement
	Definition
	Governing Value Statement
	Definition

From chapter 4, list your life's goals.

My Life Goals:

-

-

-

-

-

-

-

-

PART 2

THE VENUES
OF SELF-LEADERSHIP

6

SPIRITUAL SELF-LEADERSHIP

PERSONAL SOUL CARE

In early 1998 President Bill Clinton stood before a group representing the national clergy at a prayer breakfast being held in the East Room of the White House and uttered words that seemed to be as awkward as they were poignant. The president used the occasion to offer a personal, spiritual confession; "I have sinned," the president admitted; "There is no other way to say it." His confession was related to his illicit relationship with Monica Lewinsky and the public storm of controversy and chaos it had spawned.

Here was the most powerful man in the free world sheepishly standing before this collection of religious leaders, his face pale and drawn from weeks of enduring the accusations surrounding his most recent blunder, acting more like a boy who had been caught with his hand in the cookie jar than a world leader. It was an unapologetically spiritual moment for a publically elected government leader.

It had become clear that many people in the country were growing concerned with the president's spiritual bearing, struggling with the president's apparent lack of moral rectitude and integrity. The result was this confession, which was intended to provide the public with a window into the president's personal spiritual life that might possibly restore his constituents' sagging confidence in him as a leader. At this crucial time, it was the president's spirituality that was called on in an effort to fortify his crumbling leadership foundation.

AWKWARD NO LONGER

In today's cultural environment it is no longer awkward or uncommon to mention both spirituality and leadership in the same sentence. Even in completely irreligious business and political settings the exercise of leadership is more and more frequently being spoken of in spiritual terms. In fact the current trend is to talk about leadership as a spiritual activity, regardless of the realm in which it is exercised.

While working on this chapter at my local Barnes and Noble, I decided to conduct my own impromptu survey in the leadership/business section of the store. Within just a few minutes of hastily rifling through the crowded shelves, I was able to find numerous volumes dedicated to the exploration and discussion of the spiritual aspects of leadership. None of these books, interestingly enough, had been published by what one would consider a Christian publishing house. Among the books I discovered were titles like *Leading with Soul*, *The Stirring of the Soul in the Workplace*, *Connections between Spirit and Work*, *The Heart of an Executive: Lessons on Leadership from the Life of King David*, and *The Soul of Business*. Each of these books had been written and published within the last two years. Clearly the correlation between leadership and spirituality has become more readily recognized in recent years.

In part, I believe this renewed focus on spirituality as it relates to leaders has resulted from what seems to have been the absence

128

of moral and ethical leadership during the 1980s—what has become known as the decade of greed. Another contributing factor in recent years has no doubt been the significant and high-profile leadership failures that we have witnessed in government, business, and religious institutions. I believe it can be safely concluded that this current interest in encouraging leaders to examine and address their personal spirituality is in response to the reality that effective leadership in any realm must derive from the leader's inner life, not merely his or her skill set. Leadership is not merely the exercise of certain skills and techniques. Leadership, regardless of the realm in which it is exercised, is actually the public manifestation and application of deeply held personal values and beliefs in an effort to positively influence the corporate good. As such, leadership is rightly defined as a spiritual activity; it is the public acting out of a person's inner life—what we call soul or spirit.

LEADERSHIP FAILURES ARE SPIRITUAL FAILURES

In light of the reality that leadership is, at its most essential level, a spiritual activity, I would strongly contend that in the final analysis every leadership failure is, at its root, a spiritual issue. Regardless of whether the failure takes the shape of sexual immorality, unethical business practices, criminal activity, or any other impropriety that could lead to a leadership failure, at the core of all of these failures is the leader's inability to recognize, diagnose, and address spiritual disease of one sort or another in his life.

Thus one of the primary venues in which effective self-leadership must be consistently exercised is the venue of the leader's spiritual life, what I will call personal soul care. There is no other aspect of a leader's life that has greater impact, both positive and negative, on her exercise of leadership than the condition of her inner life.

At the risk of belaboring the issue, President Clinton's failure has been variously described as a lapse of judgment, reckless private behavior, a sexual indiscretion, and countless other euphemisms that, in the end, minimize and ignore the heart of the issue. Even as the president sought out "spiritual advisors" to help him deal with his own behavior, the media was reluctant to identify his failure in spiritual terms. And yet it is clear that above all else the president's failure as a leader has been, by his own admission, the result of his refusal to deal with deeply seated spiritual issues.

Just to clarify, it is important to note that I am not using "spiritual" here as a synonym for "religious." Religion is our attempt as human beings to address matters of the soul. Religion is the vehicle by which a person attempts to nurture and address spiritual issues. The president could have chosen to deal with his apparent spiritual needs through the vehicle of religious commitment or practice. However, I suggest that he chose instead to deal with his spiritual needs by engaging in illicit sexual activity.

Similarly, there are many spiritual leaders today who have experienced significant failure and, to a lesser degree, leadership ineffectiveness as a direct result of neglecting to exercise effective self-leadership in the venue of their own spiritual life.

In his book *Care of Souls,* psychologist David Benner suggests that careful attention to one's inner life is an indispensable prerequisite of providing leadership to others.[1] I concur with Dr. Benner's assessment. The true quality and nature of our leadership will ultimately be determined by the condition of our inner life, which, in turn, is the product of the degree to which we do or do not engage in effective personal soul care.

Unfortunately the number of spiritual leaders and pastors who do not engage in the exercise of regular personal soul care is truly disturbing. This laxity can be the precursor to serious spiritual apathy, boredom, and an absence of passion, a malady the desert fathers of the first through fourth centuries called acedia. And this can lead to significant failure as a leader.

Acedia is that place in our spiritual life where indifference reigns supreme and, as Charles Swindoll has said, "We don't even sin with passion!" Like drifting aimlessly in the strength-sapping heat of the equatorial doldrums without even the slightest breeze to ruffle the sail, acedia sucks the spiritual life out of us and we begin leading from a vacuous soul. Urban T. Holmes III calls the experience of acedia a time when the leader's spiritual life is being sustained only by the embers of a dying soul.[2] This spiritual malady can be the direct result of failing over a protracted period of time to exercise effective spiritual self-leadership. Acedia, and to a larger extent the potential for a life-crushing ministry failure, is born and nurtured in the weedy spiritual soil that is the result of neglectful personal soul care.

THE BIBLE AND PERSONAL SOUL CARE

The Scriptures are replete with admonitions for followers of Christ to give the most careful attention possible to the development, nurture, and leadership of their own inner life, which constitutes personal soul care. In fact an entire book dedicated to fully exploring the topic would not be sufficient, so I will present here only a few of the more noteworthy passages.

In Psalm 119:1–6, the psalmist writes clearly of the importance of personal soul care that can be accomplished from adequate exposure to God's Word:

> Happy are people of integrity, who follow the law of the LORD.
> Happy are those who obey his decrees and search for him with all their hearts.
> They do not compromise with evil, and they walk only in his paths.
> You have charged us to keep your commandments carefully.
> Oh, that my actions would consistently reflect your principles!
> Then I will not be disgraced when I compare my life with your commands.

Then again in verses 9 and 11 the psalmist addresses the importance of the personal purity and integrity that result from personal soul care:

131

How can a young person stay pure? By obeying your word and following its rules.

I have hidden your word in my heart, that I might not sin against you.

Clearly, inner purity, integrity, and health through frequent and consistent exposure to the sacred text are essential elements of personal soul care that must be given the utmost attention, according to this psalm.

Additionally, we know that even Jesus himself, God in human flesh, felt it vital to get away regularly from the frenetic schedule imposed by leadership for times of inner refreshment, renewal, and nurture, as well as for maintaining a clear connection between his will and the Father's. We see this pattern repeated by Jesus and throughout the Gospels.

Additionally, Jesus reserved his harshest judgment and criticism for those leaders who neglected their inner life and the practice of authentic spirituality that was able to affect their leadership from the inside out.

In Matthew 23 Jesus pronounced his infamous woes on the externally religious Pharisees, chastising them for their shallow spirituality with its emphasis on appearances.

How terrible it will be for you teachers of religious law and you Pharisees. Hypocrites! You are so careful to clean the outside of the cup and the dish, but inside you are filthy—full of greed and self-indulgence! Blind Pharisees! First wash the inside of the cup, and *then the outside will become clean, too.* How terrible it will be for you teachers of religious law and you Pharisees. Hypocrites! You are like whitewashed tombs—beautiful on the outside but filled on the inside with dead people's bones and all sorts of impurity. You try to look like upright people outwardly, but inside your hearts are filled with hypocrisy and lawlessness.

Matthew 23:25–28, emphasis mine

Evidently Jesus felt quite strongly that those who exercise spiritual leadership of others must maintain regular spiritual leadership in their own lives.

As we saw in chapter 1, Paul admonished Timothy to engage in regular personal soul care when he instructed Timothy, "Give your complete attention to these matters. Throw yourself into your tasks so that everyone will see your progress. Keep a close watch on yourself and on your teaching. Stay true to what is right, and God will save you and those who hear you" (1 Tim. 4:15–16). Paul wanted this young leader to be absorbed with personal soul care and the spiritual disciplines.

From even a cursory examination of the Bible we can see that great import is given to the need for individuals, particularly leaders, to attend to this vital area of their life and leadership.

THE PRACTICE OF REGULAR SPIRITUAL DISCIPLINES

If, as I have suggested and the Scriptures seem to substantiate, the exercise of leadership is essentially spiritual in nature, what are the ways in which we as leaders can adequately care for our souls, helping us to be effective leaders? How can we exercise self-leadership in this area of our life that appears to be the headwaters from which all of our leadership flows?

I believe there are several vital elements that must be attended to in our efforts to practice efficacious personal soul care. Though what follows is by no means an exhaustive list of disciplines or practices, it will provide the concerned and willing leader with more than sufficient resources to begin or enhance his personal soul care.

The place for the leader to begin, without doubt, is to establish a regular time in her life that is devoted to the practice of certain spiritual disciplines. The words *practice* and *discipline* should not be too quickly overlooked in the above prescription. Practice and discipline are the keys that will enable us to not only maintain personal soul care for a lifetime but also unlock the secrets that will enable us to deeply enjoy the process.

I have come by this realization in a very unlikely and non-spiritual way. There was a time when I was very interested in playing golf. As a newly ordained minister I assumed that learning to play golf was a prerequisite to successfully carrying out my ministry in a local parish setting.

In an effort to better exercise the ministerial gift of golf, I began taking lessons at a small golf shop located in a shopping center across the street from the first church in which I served as an associate pastor in southern California. Being somewhat compulsive in personality, I dedicated myself without reservation to learning and mastering this frustrating sport. I persisted in taking my lessons for two years, during which time I practiced daily—both at home, with a net I had set up, and at the local driving range. My commitment to mastering the golf swing had seemed to take on the urgency of a decidedly spiritual quest.

However, much to my dismay (and my wife's delight), I could never quite conquer this perplexing and illusive game. The golf swing always seemed unnatural and clumsy to me—especially when I did it the way I had been instructed.

Chief among my frustrations was golfing with colleagues and friends who were able to swing the golf club as if it were a natural extension of their body—like a graphite appendage wired directly to their brain! Every one of their smooth, effortless swings that I was forced to witness only served to remind me that I definitely lacked the fluidity and ease that seemed to produce the enjoyment and pleasure my friends received from playing golf.

Eventually I learned that most of the friends whose golf games I admired had been playing the game for many years. They had begun young and consistently practiced the various elements of the game, which resulted in the expertise I witnessed. Unfortunately I was a Johnny-come-lately to the game of golf but expected to enjoy the same level of ease and fluidity that had taken my friends many years to acquire. I simply got frustrated and quit too soon. I was not willing to exercise the discipline and practice necessary over an extended period of time that would have allowed my golf swing to become more natural and greatly enhance my enjoyment of the game.

When it comes to the game of golf, discipline and practice are absolutely essential to the eventual enjoyment of the sport, which will, in turn, encourage the playing of the game for many years.

I would like to suggest, with biblical support, that the spiritual disciplines involved in the practice of effective personal soul care are very similar to the game of golf. They require discipline and practice before they can be genuinely enjoyed and maintained for a lifetime.

Today the leadership landscape is strewn with the abandoned spiritual golf clubs of prayer, Scripture reading, and other disciplines, discarded by those who began the exercise of personal soul care, only to give up after several months of fruitless and joyless flailing. Like the frustrated duffer who never plays the game of golf with enough consistency and practice for it to become natural and enjoyable, many spiritual leaders give up on the practice of spiritual disciplines before they begin actually enjoying them.

Though we use the word *practice* in everyday language, we often fail to understand its implications in a spiritual context. We are quick to equate practice with simply "doing" something or engaging in an activity. However, more specifically, the word *practice,* according to the *American Heritage Dictionary* means to do or perform something habitually or customarily. It has the idea of doing something repeatedly until it becomes a habit. To practice something also means to engage in an activity until it is perfected and second nature.

Thus we say that a physician *practices* medicine and that an attorney *practices* law. This is not to suggest that they do not yet know what they are doing. Rather, it more accurately means that they have disciplined themselves to learn and have repeatedly engaged in those activities essential to the skillful performance of medical or legal care. They are experts in their field.

If activities such as swinging a golf club, shooting clay pigeons on the fly, connecting a baseball bat with a speeding fastball, or casting a delicate fly to a waiting trout require practice before they are enjoyable, then most assuredly the same is true for the disciplines we will discuss in this chapter. Our failure to understand this basic principle will certainly lead to our frustration and abstinence when it comes to the spiritual disciplines that comprise the essential elements of personal soul care.

The writer to the Hebrews speaks of the importance of practice when it comes to mastering the personal soul care that brings growth and enjoyment to the spiritual life when he writes, "But solid food is for the mature, who because of practice have their senses trained to discern good and evil" (Heb. 5:14 NASB). Similarly, Peter says, "Therefore, brethren, be all the more diligent to make certain about His calling and choosing you; for as long as you practice these things, you will never stumble" (2 Peter 1:10 NASB).

In Philippians 4, Paul seems to be alluding to the same principle when he says that he has "learned" to be content in all circumstances. The fact that it was something he had to learn implies that it was not something that came to him naturally. It no doubt required a degree of practice and discipline to remain in the settings and situations that would enable Paul to practice and acquire this spiritual discipline. It could be safely speculated that had Paul quit pursuing his life goals and Calling after his first several uncomfortable encounters with difficult times, he never would have learned this important discipline.

So it is for us when it comes to the disciplines that facilitate personal soul care. We cannot quit if we hope to have these disciplines become a natural aspect of our spiritual life and leadership. Like athletes or practitioners of any activity that requires the acquisition of a specific skill, we must stay at the disciplines until we begin to master them and they begin to become as natural to us as taking a shower, brushing our teeth, or getting dressed in the morning.

THE ELEMENTS OF EFFECTIVE SOUL CARE

Now that the importance of practice and discipline has been duly noted and established, what exactly are the disciplines that we must practice? I will suggest only those that I feel form the foundation for adequate soul care, though there are many others that are worthy of our exploration and practice.

SCRIPTURE READING

Scripture reading is the foundation on which all of the other disciplines must be built. It is essential that spiritual leaders regularly expose themselves to the Scriptures in such a way that

136

God's Word is able to be used by the Holy Spirit to mold, refine, change, inform, convict, and ultimately shape us into the image of Jesus Christ.

The primary means for spiritual growth and development is the renewing of our mind. In Romans 12:2 the apostle Paul explains that it is through the transforming of our minds that God is able to change us. Every behavior, whether good or bad, begins in our mind. It is our thinking that must be changed if we are ever to change the way we live and lead. And the primary agent of this type of transformation is the inspired Word of God, skillfully wielded by the Holy Spirit, as we deliberately expose ourselves to it for that express purpose.

Though it is important that we read the Scriptures for information and study, that is not the kind of reading I am advocating here as a discipline of personal soul care. The Scripture reading of soul care is done with the primary purpose of allowing our inner person to be transformed. It is reading the Scripture to experience the mind and heart of God. The Scripture reading that is done for the purpose of soul care is done slowly, expectantly, and repeatedly. It is what the church fathers called *lectio divina,* the careful digesting of the scriptural truths and principles being read. It is reading in such a way as to hear what the Spirit is saying to us. It is allowing the word to truly "live" in us or, as Paul told the Colossians, "Let the words of Christ, in all their richness, live in your hearts and make you wise" (Col. 3:16).

In an effort to enhance our ability to hear what God is saying to us and allow us to absorb the principles and truths he has for us, I believe it is best to do our Scripture reading in a version of the Bible that is different from the one we use for regular study and preparation for teaching. I have found that the New Living Translation is excellent for this, as is *The Message* by Eugene Peterson.

The reason for such a change in translation is to keep us from viewing every passage we read as a possible sermon or lesson outline. When I try to do my Scripture reading in the translation I study in and preach from, I find myself approaching each text as a potential sermon—it is almost instinctive now after fifteen years. I subconsciously begin outlining the text and mentally approach it in a way that is not the most conducive to personal soul care.

137

I realize that everyone is different and that what works for me may not work for you. If you have not tried this method of bringing freshness to your reading of Scripture, however, I strongly suggest that you give it a try.

Regardless of the translation you choose to use, this kind of reading must be done in solitude and silence. Solitude means that you are alone and silence means that you are alone in a quiet place that will foster reflection and thought without distraction or disturbance. It is not possible to effectively engage in this kind of reading with the television on in the background or with people scurrying all around. That would be akin to attempting to enter into a meaningful conversation with a loved one while watching television. Though many people try to do this, the usual result is poor communication and an unsatisfying relationship. So it is in our relationship with God as well. Effective personal soul care must begin with the attentive reading of Scripture.

PRAYER

Closely related to Scripture reading is the discipline of prayer. Unfortunately, to my way of thinking, prayer has been the recipient of a bad rap when it comes to the way it is perceived by today's high-octane spiritual leaders, who often see it as a "nonproductive" activity. For many, prayer is equated with long, silent hours kneeling at some easy chair, spending more time fending off sleep and feeling guilty for it than engaging in an intimate, stimulating, conversational relationship with God.

For those brought up in the church, prayer has taken on many different images and stereotypes, most of them less than exciting, which do not contribute to our desire to make prayer a consistent activity in our list of spiritual disciplines.

Having been reared in the church, I am very familiar with the battle involved in actively engaging in prayer that is both meaningful and effective. However, though it may very well be a battle, it is a battle well worth the waging and winning. Few things will keep us on course in the exercise of our leadership and facilitate the care of our soul as much as meaningful prayer when engaged in consistently.

I have found some of my most effective prayer times to be built around my Scripture reading. It seems to take place effortlessly if I have indeed engaged in effective Scripture reading as described above. After forty-five minutes reflecting on a portion of Scripture, regardless of its genre or where it is found in the Bible, I have found that the Holy Spirit stirs me to prayer that is wholly natural and without design on my part.

The prayer that is prompted by Scripture inevitably leads me to times of confession, intercession, adoration, worship, and thanksgiving, among other expressions that I could never have contrived on my own. However, these times are most often without formal structure, flowing from confession to thanksgiving, intercession to adoration, and back again to confession, all within the same prayer time. For those of us used to the helpful acronym ACTS (adoration, confession, thanksgiving, supplication) or some other preformatted prayer time, this can be a prayer experience that may well take some getting used to. But again, it is an effort well worth making.

Who can lead us into meaningful prayer better than the Holy Spirit? The apostle Paul, in Romans 8:26–27, tells us that the Holy Spirit helps us know what we should pray for and how we should pray. The reality is we don't know how to pray as we should. Those of us who are honest enough to admit it know how futile our best efforts often are, even as people who have been followers of Christ for many years. There must be an easier and better way!

Speaking with and listening to our Father and spending time in his refreshing presence should not make us miserable! Prayer is not intended to be a form of spiritual torture, designed to separate the saints from those of shallow soul. It is, I believe, intended by God to be our lifeline. Prayer should be something that is taking place within us almost involuntarily, like breathing.

My eight-year-old son, Sammy, like my other three children, is the joy of my life. I can just look at him and burst with joy on the inside (and it almost always seeps to the outside in the form of a big smile)! Well, Sammy is constantly talking to me. Whenever we are together, regardless of what I might be attempting to do, Sammy is there at my side, just chatting away. Often he expects no answer or serious dialogue. I think he simply finds comfort and joy in talking to me. He talks about his school day; he talks about a book he's read; he chatters about a friend at school or an activity that is coming up; Sammy tells me about things that make him mad and people who have hurt his feelings—you name it and Sammy talks about it.

As his father, there is nothing I enjoy more than hearing Sammy talk to me. Even if I'm writing or studying, Sammy's little voice, with his unique pronunciation of certain words, has never once bored me. I love him. And I love to hear him chatter. I have learned how to be a better dad to Sammy as a result of these times of unplanned, unstructured conversation. I have learned what concerns him and what he is scared of. I have discovered what he likes and what he wants, where he wants to go, and the places he hopes to avoid. Sammy knows how to talk to his dad.

I can't imagine what would happen to these precious times if I handed Sammy a list of topics to be discussed during our times together or a structured guide on how to proceed on these occasions. It would kill them. The formality and structure would rob these times of their spontaneity and enjoyment—they would become more like work for both of us. In fact, more than likely, Sammy would simply stop talking. And yet that is exactly how we try to talk to our Heavenly Father. Is it any wonder these talks are painful and we try to avoid them? What we need to do is approach our Heavenly Father much more naturally, under the skillful guidance of the Holy Spirit, rather than as if we are approaching a high-pressure negotiation with an adversary or competitor who needs softening up and convincing.

Another way that I have found prayer to be much more effective and meaningful for me is to write prayers in my journal (I will discuss journaling later). I simply allow my prayers to flow from my heart and onto the page, again prompted by my time in Scripture and under the guidance of the Holy Spirit. In all honesty, there are times when these written prayers seem nothing more than an endless stream of simple chatter with God—certainly nothing approaching good or even interesting writing. And yet those prayers are heartfelt and reflect the state of my soul at that point in time. I don't think God minds. I don't believe he's concerned with my spelling or grammar. Sentence fragments and misplaced subjects mean nothing to him as my prayers spill onto the page. I am convinced that he is simply glad to be hearing from me about those things that concern, frighten, worry, and excite me. He is my Father and he loves and, yes, even delights in me!

For the more compulsive personalities among us, it is important that we not critique our written prayers or succumb to the temptation to go back and correct them. We must allow them to stand as a testament to time spent in personal relationship with our Heavenly Father—we don't have to be perfect for him—we need only to be consciously present with him, and journaling our prayers allows that to take place.

In addition to my free-form praying, which flows out of my Scripture reading and my prayer journaling, I have found a set of books titled *Face to Face,* by Kenneth Boa, to be extremely helpful in facilitating meaningful times of prayer. There are two companion volumes in this series; volume one is *Praying the Scriptures for Spiritual Growth,* and the other is *Praying the Scriptures for Intimate Worship.*[3] Both of these prayer guides are built entirely on the concept of allowing the Holy Spirit to prompt a response from us in the form of prayer. If you are just beginning to practice the discipline of prayer, or trying to break away from methods of prayer that have proven fruitless, I highly recommend these two little guides.

In the end, it is important to remember that prayer is everything we engage in that increases our awareness of God.[4] When Jesus taught his disciples to pray, it was really quite simple. God in human flesh taught his children how to pray in one brief paragraph (see Matt. 6:9–13). Yet, like most everything else we human beings become involved with, we have transformed prayer into a complex, difficult, and tiring exercise that has spawned countless "how to" volumes that require weeks to read. If we are serious about engaging in personal soul care that will endure, it is essential that we recapture a simple yet profound prayer life that will motivate us to pray.

141

Journaling as a spiritual discipline has been an essential element of personal soul care for centuries. From the Old Testament kings David and Solomon to the desert fathers as well as today's earnest disciples, writing a journal has been an essential means to the end of spiritual growth and personal soul care.

In my first book, *Overcoming the Dark Side of Leadership,* written with Gary McIntosh, I wrote at length about the vital role journaling plays in the maintenance of God-honoring leadership and the promotion of personal growth.

> The practice of keeping a journal involves putting one's life down on paper . . . as a clarifying process: "Who am I? What am I doing and why? How do I feel about my life, my world? In what ways am I growing or changing?"
>
> If there is one thing leaders need as they pursue self-knowledge and understanding, it is the ability to clarify the fears, motives, insecurities, and other emotions that lurk deep beneath the surface of their public leadership persona. Keeping a journal forces us to be honest with ourselves. It is possibly the only place where we can truly be ourselves, warts and all. In our journal we can finally explore our inner rumblings and give definition and shape to them. The safe confines of our journal can help us admit to feelings of jealousy, selfishness, and pride. Within these therapeutic pages we can feel free to identify those inner urges and compulsions that drive us. The simple act of placing them on paper, in black and white, reduces their power over us to some degree.
>
> . . . However, your journal will only be helpful to the degree that you are honest with yourself. It is important to remember as you keep a journal that the river of self-deceit and denial runs so deep and swift that your initial attempts to ford it may end in getting swept away by the current. There will be a constant temptation to paint yourself in the most favorable light. The urge will be strong to simply leave out some of your uglier and more negative behaviors and actions. When you succumb to these urges, you are being swept away by the current of self-denial and deceit. Just the act of journaling will not be helpful if you cannot be honest and probe your inner recesses. But rather than becoming dis-

couraged and quitting, you need to persist until you are finally able to walk through the depths.[5]

PERSONAL RETREAT

A final discipline that I would like to suggest is that of engaging in regular times of personal retreat. This discipline has its roots in the life of Jesus himself. In the Gospels we find numerous accounts of Jesus escaping the frenzy and chaos often created by effective public ministry by stealing away to a remote place for a time of reflection, prayer, rest, and empowerment. Often these times of retreat seemed to occur either immediately before or immediately after times of intense and successful ministry.

It is easy for us to think that when things are going well and we are seeing encouraging ministry successes that we do not need a break. When positive events are taking place, it is often difficult to step away for a day or two; we fear losing the momentum that has built up. But wise spiritual leaders realize that success produces its own forms of stress and anxiety—often more insidious than the stress that results from struggles in ministry. If we fail to take the breaks necessary to maintain our balance, even overwhelming ministry success can produce crippling spiritual failure.

This is not to suggest that all personal retreats will be times of existential bliss and divine mountaintop experiences. To the contrary, some of our retreats will involve a certain measure of emotional anguish and spiritual challenge as we wrestle with God for his direction and insight. That being said, these times of wrestling with God can also, paradoxically, prove to be life-giving times that refuel our passion for God and the ministry to which he has called us.

The need for personal retreat was a fundamental aspect of public life and leadership that Jesus was quite aware of and took seriously. In Matthew's Gospel, at the very beginning of Jesus' public ministry, we read that he retreated to the wilderness to be alone with his Heavenly Father in preparation for public ministry. This was a time of intense spiritual testing and struggle. Yet at the same time it was this time of struggle in personal retreat that prepared our Lord for his abundantly effective ministry.

143

At other times, Jesus retreated to prepare himself for important decisions that had to be made, as when he selected his disciples. When faced with difficult circumstances, such as his impending encounter with the cross, Jesus sought out time alone to be with his Heavenly Father and gain the strength necessary to endure the trial. Time and again Jesus removed himself from the company of others and the hectic activity of daily life to regain his perspective for ministry and renew his eternal focus.

If Jesus found it necessary to engage regularly in this discipline, how much more vital should it be for us? And yet few of today's leaders are willing to consistently invest in this exercise that has proven itself over the centuries to yield invaluable returns.

There are several reasons why the discipline of personal retreat is so easily neglected. First, it requires time. Time is one of the twenty-first century's most valuable commodities, and not many are willing to exchange it for something the worth of which they consider dubious at best. A second reason this discipline is difficult is that many people have no idea where to go for such a time of prayer and reflection. Finally, not knowing what exactly to do on a personal retreat can serve as another reason for not making it a regular part of one's routine.

I have found that the time I spend in personal retreat is the time that provides the greatest return for my life. If time is a valuable commodity, then surely we should want to invest it in such a way that it provides us with a meaningful return. During my times of retreat, without any formal study or specifically targeted thought, God has led me to the topics and issues that he would like me to cover in my preaching. If, as a pastor, you have ever found yourself vainly laboring over the latest Max Lucado book or analyzing current events in an effort to distill them into a new sermon series you can preach, you know how valuable it is to receive those insights that give specific direction in this area.

It is in my times of personal retreat that I am often made aware of my need to slow down and enjoy life more as opposed to living and working at a breakneck pace. Fortunately, just about the time I find myself kicking back into compulsive high gear, it is time once again for my monthly retreat and I am given the opportunity to regain my balance before my compulsivity causes me to spiral out of control.

There are two basic issues that must be settled before we can begin the discipline of personal retreat—where will we go and what will we do?

Surprisingly, there are many places we can go that will facilitate a meaningful time of retreat. I have made a habit of finding the local monasteries and retreat centers in whatever place I am ministering. I have lived in places as diverse as the vast Los Angeles basin in southern California and Sioux Falls, South Dakota, with stops in between, and have never had a problem locating adequate retreat facilities. In fact, in most of these places, including Sioux Falls, I have found outstanding retreat centers within ninety minutes of where I live. Not only have these facilities been reasonably priced (most require only a small donation), but they have also been extremely comfortable. While in southern California, I frequented the Saint Andrews Abbey, tucked away at the base of the gorgeous San Gabriel Mountains. St. Andrews provided private quarters, an inviting central lodge, a chapel where I was welcome to worship with the monks, as well as miles of walking trails for times of reflection and meditation.

Currently, I am going to Blue Cloud Abbey, about an hour north of my home in Sioux Falls. This monastery provides quaint and comfortable private cabins, what they call "prayer cottages," which are fully furnished and well stocked. Additionally, these small cottages have no electricity or running water, which enhances one's ability to get away from it all and focus wholly on God. Regardless of where I have lived, I have always been able to find great retreat locations if I have been willing to ask others and look around myself.[6]

Another option for the more adventurous leader is to find a good location to set up a tent and retreat to the wilderness. I have also done this and found it to be very constructive and conducive to a meaningful time of retreat.

It is equally important to think about where we should *not* take a retreat. I personally do not recommend attempting to retreat in a hotel or motel. These are too much like home and have too many distractions and temptations to be good retreat centers. The telephone and television will serve as constant temptations to most of us in one way or another. Whether the temptation is to hook up our laptop and check our e-mail or relax in the evening while watching CNN, the temptations offered by today's hotels and motels will be difficult to resist for most modern ministers.

And most hotels and motels are not in settings where there are trails to hike and nature to enjoy. These are often the most memorable parts of my retreats. Hotels and motels will also be much more expensive than the types of retreat centers I recommend.

Another definite no-no when it comes to choosing a retreat center is to stay at home. Regardless of your home situation, staying at home will definitely *not* promote a meaningful time of retreat. Even if you have no children at home and your spouse works, staying at home in an effort to conduct a personal retreat will be both ineffective and ultimately discouraging. When we are at home, virtually everything we lay our eyes on evokes a memory or serves as a reminder of things left undone that have a very high likelihood of derailing our good intentions. I firmly believe, as a result of personal trial and error, that finding a good retreat center is critical to this discipline and our willingness to practice it for a lifetime.

In addition to location, we must answer the question, What will I do once I have found a suitable site? I like to think of my personal retreats as an extension of my daily disciplines. For the most part, I follow the same personal liturgy during retreat that I do in my time of disciplines at home, except that I am able to go through several cycles throughout the day while on retreat.

After arriving at the retreat site, I unpack and get situated in my room or cabin. Once I have settled in, I speak with the retreat master or person in charge to learn where different facilities are and what the community's schedule is for morning prayer, noon prayer, vespers, as well as any other unique daily rhythms for that community. After these details are taken care of, I begin my time of retreat with an hour spent in silence, simply allowing myself to unwind and refocus on God and the reason I am in this

146

new place. After my time of silence, I spend time reading Scripture in the manner previously mentioned and allow it to flow into a time of prayer and meditation. From here I move to a time of devotional reading, utilizing brief readings by the likes of Henri Nouwen, Evelyn Underhill, Urban T. Holmes, Eugene Peterson, C. S. Lewis, and others who have written in the contemplative genre. After this time of reading, I generally reflect on all that I've done so far (in my Scripture reading, prayer, and devotional reading) and then journal in response to what I sense God is saying to me.

After journaling, I will go for a hike or walk, allowing the preceding time spent in Scripture, prayer, and journaling to "percolate" as I walk. After my hike, I take time for a nap and then begin my liturgical cycle all over again. On a twenty-four-hour retreat I usually experience at least three of these cycles, concluding my retreat with the celebration of communion.

A tool that I highly recommend for spiritual leaders who desire to integrate the discipline of personal retreat into their personal soul care is the volume *A Guide to Prayer for Ministers and Other Servants* by Norman Shawchuck and Ruben Job. At the end of this guide are models and themes for twelve monthly personal retreats that I have found extremely helpful.

Obstacles to Effective Soul Care

No matter how well intentioned we are in our efforts to consistently practice the spiritual disciplines as a nonnegotiable element of our life and leadership, we will face countless obstacles that will threaten to derail our best efforts.

Busyness

For driven, aggressive leaders who tend to be more task oriented than people oriented, busyness will be the chief obstacle that threatens to keep us from making the consistent practice of spiritual disciplines a part of our life.

The reality is that busyness is both the chief obstacle to practicing personal soul care as well as the prime symptom of our failure to do so. Often we allow ourselves to be consumed by busyness precisely so that we will not have to confront the shallowness of soul that has resulted from our failure to exercise effective spiritual self-leadership.

Even recognizing this reality, the fact remains that there is nothing more difficult to do when we are in the middle of an incredibly busy and productive leadership schedule than taking the time necessary to spend the better part of two days away in reflection and prayer. A common temptation during these times is to say, "When things slow down, then I'll get away for retreat." But it is during these times that we most need to maintain our discipline and make our personal retreat a priority.

FRUSTRATION

Another obstacle that will confront us is the temptation to give up on our disciplines too soon, before we are able to realize the positive benefit they will bring to our life and leadership. It is easy to become frustrated when we fail to see any immediate tangible benefits from our exercise of personal soul care. It is easy to think that our time might be more wisely invested in more "productive" pursuits. However, the spiritual disciplines are much like antibiotics. When our physician prescribes a course of antibiotics to fight an infection that is the source of physical pain and discomfort, he is always careful to tell us to finish all of the medicine. You see, antibiotics don't generally work overnight. It takes time for the right therapeutic level to be achieved, which will then allow the drug to be effective in eliminating the infection that is the cause of our pain. If, after taking our antibiotic for two days, we don't experience the results we desire and quit taking it, we will never realize the potential benefit it offers. We must keep taking the medicine consistently, even when we do not feel or see any immediate benefit.

It is the same with the spiritual disciplines. It takes some time before the prescribed course of Scripture, prayer, journaling, and personal retreat, which are all a part of effective personal soul

148

care, begins delivering the benefits of which it is capable. We simply must not become frustrated and quit before reaping the rewards of our efforts.

LAZINESS

Laziness will also conspire with our weaker self to keep us from the practice of these disciplines. Laziness will tempt us to stay in bed for an extra hour rather than get up and engage in our disciplines.

One of the greatest cultivators of laziness for almost anyone is television. Time spent with the television is, for the most part, unproductive time. Granted, educational and inspiring programs are offered occasionally, but these, unfortunately, are the exception rather than the rule. Excessive television watching spawns laziness. Any time spent in front of the television is time that could be spent in the exercise of spiritual disciplines. And it could be that the best time for you to engage in your disciplines is in the evening while others in the family are watching television or busy with their own activities. This is especially true if you find it impossible to rouse yourself out of bed at 5 A.M. Taking some time in the evening for spiritual disciplines should still leave you with the time you need to interact with your family before everyone goes to bed.

BATTLING THE OBSTACLES

The obstacles we will face as we undertake spiritual disciplines are as numerous and diverse as the individuals who seek to overcome them. Each of us will no doubt have our own unique nemesis to conquer in this battle, but there is some comfort in knowing that we all will have to constantly overcome numerous obstacles if we are to engage in meaningful personal soul care. But, after all, that is what being a transformational leader is all about.

Leading change is never easy. Overcoming obstacles to see positive movement and progress in the life of our organization and the people who comprise it is always challenging. At the same time, the status quo constantly and actively resists the changes that we envision and attempt. But again, isn't that what leading is all about—exercising the influence necessary to make productive changes to existing paradigms?

Effective self-leadership means that we are able to identify where changes in our life are needed and then make those changes, increasing the quality of our life as a leader. If we can't change our personal paradigm to incorporate the consistent and meaningful practice of the spiritual disciplines in our life, I would contend that we have no business attempting to lead other people or organizations to make difficult changes.

A SELF-LEADERSHIP WORKSHOP

1. List your life values from your personal constitution, following chapter 5, that fall into the venue of Spiritual Self-Leadership, for example: Maintain a growing conversational relationship with God; build the church of Jesus Christ; influence others to pursue a growing relationship with God; maintain a daily time of solitude for the purpose of spiritual growth.

My Spiritual Self-Leadership Values

-
-
-
-
-

2. Based on the above values, which of the Elements of Effective Soul Care, given on pages 136–47, would be the most helpful in facilitating your ability to live out these values on a consistent basis?

Top Two	
Second Two	

3. Now take time to write down how you will begin practicing this coming week the top two elements you listed above. First, I give you an example:

Element of Soul Care	Action to Take
Regular Scripture Reading	I will implement a schedule of daily Scripture reading; 15–30 minutes per day.
Personal Retreat	Four times a year I will take at least one day to "be silent and listen" to God. Then one time a year I'll spend an extended period of time in solitude.

Element of Soul Care	Action to Take

151

7

PHYSICAL SELF-LEADERSHIP

PERSONAL RESOURCE MANAGEMENT

Les was a gifted leader. To state it more accurately, Les was actually one of those rare individuals who possess more than their fair share of both natural talent and spiritual giftedness. While some gifted leaders are highly talented in the technical aspects of leadership (e.g., master planning, forecasting, public communication skills) and others are blessed in people skills, Les had it all.

During his early years of leadership, Les skyrocketed through the upper ranks of the nonprofit Christian service organization for which he worked. Beginning right out of graduate school, he was an executive vice president within five years of joining this well-known team of Christian leaders.

But while Les had all of the tools and a track record of effectiveness, his ministry success was cut prematurely short. You see, the one thing that Les had never learned as a leader was his need to exercise self-leadership over his physical body, what I call personal resource management.

153

At the relatively young age of forty, Les was at least seventy-five pounds overweight. His blood pressure was absolutely out of control and had become literally life threatening. Additionally, he suffered from a nagging case of asthma, the symptoms of which were greatly exacerbated by the extra weight he was carrying and his high blood pressure.

Les's wife, gravely concerned by his poor physical health and his apparent apathy concerning it, constantly encouraged him to lose his weight and gain an increased measure of physical fitness; but it seemed that Les always had a ready excuse and a humorous quip to deflect the seriousness of her requests. Exercising his sizable leadership gifts in effective ministry was always more important to Les than were the tasks required to reduce his weight and improve his health.

His poor physical condition was not only a drain on Les's health, it was also the topic of countless jokes and comments shared among his colleagues and those whom he counted among his closest friends. In fact Les was often quick to join in the joking and frequently engaged in self-effacing humor regarding his weight when he spoke publicly. However, truth be known, his friends weren't joking in private. Among themselves they shared a serious concern for their friend—a concern that they too freely shared with Les.

Though Les made several unenthusiastic attempts to lose the pounds and maintain a regular exercise program, he was never quite able to keep it going—it never became for him a way of life but was always an attempt to apply a quick fix to a complex problem.

Interestingly, and quite paradoxically, applying quick fixes to complex problems was something Les abhorred when it came to dealing with organizational and ministry problems. Sadly Les was never quite able to exercise the same expert degree of leadership over his own physical life that he so skillfully exercised in his avocation.

Just days shy of his forty-first birthday Les and his family were at a regional park enjoying an early birthday celebration. After their barbecue birthday meal of Polish sausage, potato salad, pork and beans, and Les's favorite homemade ice cream for dessert,

154

Les's family challenged the family celebrating with them to a friendly game of volleyball.

After thirty or more minutes of mildly strenuous competition—at least enough for Les to have broken a sweat—Les complained to his wife of a severe crushing sensation on his chest. They both were quick to write off the sensation as heartburn—the result of one too many Polish sausages. The families resumed their friendly fight for volleyball supremacy. Moments later Les let out a dull moan and crumpled to the sand as if someone had let the air out of his body, eyes wide open with knowing fear. Les's ministry colleague, who had moments earlier spiked a winner right through Les's parted legs, was now furiously dialing 911 on his cell phone. To everyone's horror, Les was dead before the paramedics could arrive. His thirty-five-year-old wife was left without a husband. Les's sixteen-year-old daughter and twin twelve-year-old sons had been robbed of a dad. And an incredible resource and talent had been lost to God's kingdom work, primarily because of a failure to exercise serious and effective physical self-leadership.

A Resource for Ministry

I am sure that every person reading this book knows a "Les" who is actively engaged in leadership. In fact maybe you would have to reluctantly admit that *you* are a Les.

Without a doubt, one of the most difficult venues for us as leaders to exercise effective and consistent self-leadership is our physical body. Our physical health is one of those important, but generally not urgent, areas of life—what Stephen Covey[1] would label a Quadrant 2 issue—that we can ignore, neglect, and even abuse for a long period of time before the consequential chickens come home to roost. And, oddly enough, it is often highly effective leaders, both male and female, who find themselves caught in this leadership conundrum. Why is it that those who are strong leaders can't seem to give effective leadership to this vital area of their own life? Why is it that these high-octane leaders fail to see the primal connection between their physical body and their soul, their health and the exercise of holistic leadership, their physical life and their professional leadership?

I contend that one of the primary reasons (though there are doubtless myriad reasons) is because exercise and the care of one's physical body is not generally seen as a spiritual issue. You may be thinking, "Come on, everyone knows that our body is the temple of the Holy Spirit! You're exaggerating!"

If, as some readers may be silently asserting at this point, the vital link between our physical body and our spiritual well-being is known to have great significance in our exercise of effective leadership, why then is it not a subject taught to spiritual leaders in seminary?

During three years of seminary and another six chasing my doctorate, I never once was given the opportunity to attend a course in which the focus was the spiritual significance of physical fitness and the maintenance of health as those issues relate to ministry and spiritual leadership. During all of those years, I cannot even recall the mention of the physical body's importance as a tool and resource for ministry.

Some may say that this connection is an inherent aspect of any leadership discussion—a clear no-brainer. Others may well say that it is simply understood, something of which every leader is naturally aware. However, I would say that such reasoning is unfounded and unsupported by reality.

PEOPLE OF THE POTLUCK

In all of my years attending and serving the church, which now amounts to more than thirty years, I have never once been to a church meal that encouraged and actually facilitated healthy eating. Every potluck table I have ever negotiated was loaded down with fried chicken, casseroles oozing with fat, 500-calorie desserts, and the constant call of the acting host or hostess (often the pastor) to return for more.

Not that there is anything wrong with eating together as God's people and enjoying the food we eat. It is just that the subliminal message the potluck table seems to communicate to many is that engaging in gluttony is all right so long as it is done within the context of Christian fellowship.

Now before you come unglued by my depiction of the church potluck as the harlot of gluttony that slyly seduces unsuspecting Christian leaders, let me say I may have purposely overstated my case for effect. But I do believe that it is symptomatic of the way the church has neglected the spiritual importance of healthy nutrition and the effective, consistent exercise of physical self-leadership, which, in turn, will result in a lifetime of personal resource management.

The Bible and Our Body

Somewhere during the evolution of the evangelical movement we lost our connection with the body. This is not to suggest that we have ceased to focus on our bodies. Quite to the contrary, we have become obsessively focused on our bodies: how they look, the shape they take, what they can and cannot do, and how they compare to the bodies our popular culture parades before us.

The disconnect I am speaking about is how we have seemingly lost the connection between our body and our soul. It seems that modern evangelicals have forgotten (or are purposely ignoring) the biblical reality that God cares deeply about our bodies—they were created for him. In 1 Corinthians 6:13, the apostle Paul says, "But our bodies were not made for sexual immorality. They were made for the Lord, and the Lord cares about our bodies." Later in that same chapter Paul admonishes, "Don't you realize that your bodies are actually parts of Christ?" (v. 15). I believe the same question could, and should, be asked of us and by us on a regular basis as those entrusted with leadership.

If we believe, as Scripture clearly states, that our bodies are literally the residence of the Holy Spirit of the living God, we must admit that they are supremely important aspects of our spirituality and leadership. In fact just as important as our spiritual self-leadership is the self-leadership we exercise in the realm of our physical body.

157

Again Paul reminds us, "You do not belong to yourself, for God bought you with a high price. So you must honor God with your body" (1 Cor. 6:19–20). It is not just our spirit God is concerned with, he wants us to use our physical bodies to serve and glorify him.

Because the apostle Paul clearly understood the spiritual importance of his physical body and the role it played in the effective exercise of his leadership, the fleshing out of his values, and the realization of his life goals, he was serious about the exercise of physical self-leadership. He was very aware, especially in his day when medical care was rare and marginally efficacious at best, that failure to care adequately for his physical body could jeopardize his entire life mission. As a result, he was careful to give self-leadership to the venue of his body. Paul says, "So I run straight to the goal with purpose in every step. I am not like a boxer who misses his punches. I discipline [there's that pesky word again] my body like an athlete, training it to do what it should. Otherwise, I fear that after preaching to others I myself might be disqualified" (1 Cor. 9:26–27). The great apostle was painfully aware of the ways an uncontrolled body could ruin the work he was doing and disqualify him as a leader.

Additionally, not only does our physical body have spiritual significance and importance here and now, the Scripture teaches that our bodies will one day be transformed, as was the body of our Lord. Our present bodies will not be destroyed forever but will be restored and transformed into glorified bodies. As with the resurrected body of Jesus, I believe it safe to surmise that our restored, glorified bodies will bear some physical resemblance to our current bodies.

If all of this is true, why is it that we as Christians are often guilty of not only demeaning the physical body, but also neglecting it and effectively eliminating it as an essential element of holistic spirituality? As leaders we must model the biblical teaching as it relates to our body just as we obey scriptural injunctions directed at every other aspect of our life. We of all people should take seriously the need for health and physical fitness—not only as an example to those we lead but also in recognition that our body is the only tool we have with which to carry out the mission we have been given by God. Without a healthy and mobile physical body, our ability to lead is greatly reduced.

As always, however, there are exceptions. I think of Joni Eareckson Tada and the profound impact her leadership and teaching has had on Christendom. In spite of the fact that her body is greatly impaired, she still exercises superinfluential leadership. But Joni's case does not negate the point that I am trying to make. Her impairment is not the result of shoddy or neglectful physical self-leadership, but rather the result of a tragic accident over which she had no control. There is a difference. And when one looks at Joni it is obvious that she takes care of her physical body—a task made all the more difficult and challenging by her condition. She is an example of one who exercises effective physical self-leadership.

Consider for a moment the discipline it would require to be a public leader and speaker if you were bound to a wheelchair. The reality is that Joni Eareckson Tada accomplishes more than do many people whose bodies are free of any limitations—she must exercise incredible self-leadership in this area of her life. Her accomplishments are testament to the fact that she has mastered her body as the apostle Paul had.

As with everything, however, balance is the key. I am not advocating fixation on our body and elevating its importance out of balance with the other aspects of our life in Christ. We should not confuse the responsible self-leadership of our body with the fanaticism and body obsession that has taken root in our culture. Effective physical self-leadership does not mean that we strive to look like a fashion model or dress like a Hollywood star. It simply means that we give the same degree and intensity of attention to leading our life in this area as we do in those areas that are often considered more spiritual in nature.

THE ELEMENTS OF PHYSICAL SELF-LEADERSHIP

In a recent issue of *USA Today* it was reported in a special section that physicians are in the process of actually developing the resources necessary to begin writing exercise prescriptions for conditions from heart disease to diabetes and other health problems.[2] Modern medical science is learning that much of what ails us as human beings is the result of failing to care for this physical resource we have been given. As a result, the medical community is once again recognizing that the best long-term prescription for regaining good physical condition is by renewing the proactive and consistent care of our body through exercise and nutrition.

Two major elements comprise effective self-leadership in the venue of the body: physical resource management and personal recreation and rest. I am convinced that each of these elements must be given equal attention if we are to give leadership to this area of our life.

PHYSICAL RESOURCE MANAGEMENT

One of the keys to taking seriously the need to exercise leadership in this area of our life is the understanding of our physical body and its health as a limited, nonrenewable resource. We need to understand that every decision we make that impacts our body either enhances and maximizes this resource God has given us or diminishes and depletes it. Each of us has only one body and a base level of physical health. Through our actions and decisions, we have the ability to invest in our body and see that we build on the health base that we have been given, thus enhancing our physical condition or, to the contrary, our decisions can erode our health base and marginalize our physical condition, thus reducing the likelihood of long-term leadership effectiveness.

At the most fundamental level there are four major components to our physical resource management: diet and nutrition, weight management, physical fitness, and ongoing medical care. We will look briefly at each of these components and identify some specific steps for managing them well.

Diet and Nutrition

Today we are seeing large numbers of Americans plagued by poor diet and nutrition. According to recent studies and reports by numerous organizations and agencies, the United States is home to the fattest population on the planet. Though we will talk more about this in the section on weight management, it is essential that it at least be mentioned in our discussion of diet and nutrition. It is our weight that reports to those around us how well we are doing in the area of our diet and nutrition—it is one of our personal practices that cannot be hidden from view—it is evident in the shape and condition of our body. There are, of course, some individuals with naturally rapid metabolism and generous genes who can have atrocious diet and nutrition habits, yet are not overweight. Still, their poor nutrition will be reflected in their overall health.

I am convinced that one of the most crucial areas of physical self-leadership must be this component of diet and nutrition. Before we can be successful in this area, it is important that we change the way we view food. Too often eating food is viewed almost exclusively as a recreational activity or something to be done for enjoyment. Many people today have developed the habit of using food as a drug. When they are feeling depressed, they use the drug of food to gain temporary relief from their feelings of depression. When feeling happy and excited, food is often used as an expression of that mood. When some exciting achievement has been accomplished, food is often the substance of choice used to celebrate the achievement with family and friends.

In Christian circles, as was mentioned earlier in this chapter, food is often used as the center of what we have come to know as fellowship. Often, if we are honest, our fellowship is simply an excuse to eat. Think about it; how many people do you believe would attend a fellowship event in your church if there were absolutely no food involved? What if the advertised focus of such an event were solely the sharing of what God had been doing in the lives of the attendees and nourishing one another spiritually? What if, rather than focusing on food, we focused on the sharing of scriptural truths and insights that God had been using to impact our lives and help us mature in the faith? How well would such a function be attended? The sad reality is that without food as the subliminal attraction and focus of our fellowship meetings, we in the church would have precious little fellowship.

161

Much of this is the result of a distorted view of food and nutrition. Before we can effectively provide physical self-leadership for ourselves, we must begin to view food as the fuel God has provided to sustain our body and keep it functioning at peak performance. Food and the nutrients it provides our body is what gas, oil, coolant, and brake fluid are to a car. When any of them are missing, the overall function of the vehicle is impaired and, in extreme cases, the result is catastrophic—causing the machine to shut down altogether.

If you have not been exercising good leadership in this area of your life, the place to begin is with a complete physical and blood workup. It is important, before you begin filling your body with all sorts of supplements and following wacky diets in an effort to make up for lost time, that you learn what your body needs. From a proper blood workup you can learn what nutrients you are lacking and at the same time discover those areas where you need to reduce and more closely monitor your intake. Do you need more iron or calcium but need to reduce your intake of fat? Is your cholesterol level too high? These are the things you must know before you can engage in physical self-leadership.

Next, I recommend highly that you develop the discipline of daily recording the fuel you put in your body. Consider it a journal that reflects your physical journey just as your spiritual journal records your spiritual journey. By keeping a food journal you can more effectively monitor your eating patterns and identify bad habits before they become established. Again, similar to spiritual journaling and confessing your specific sins in writing, recording everything you put in your mouth and why you do it can be quite a revealing and sobering exercise. Without doubt, ignorance is our greatest enemy in the battle to provide self-leadership in this vital area. If we are unaware of how poor our health is and we remain ignorant of patterns in our eating, we have no motivation to change and no idea how we should change. I am absolutely convinced that the way we eat and fuel the body God has given us is a deeply spiritual issue that matters to him a great deal.

There are numerous places in Scripture where God condemns the abuse of food, or gluttony, in the strongest terms. The Hebrew word most frequently used for gluttony has the root meaning of being shaky or loose. It is the picture of a person who is unstable and uncontrolled in his living. Gluttony was strongly associated with moral looseness and debauchery. To be gluttonous in one's relationship with food was to be considered "riotous" and unruly.[3]

In Proverbs gluttony is equated with a disgraceful lifestyle and a way of life that leads to poverty and ruin. The wisdom writer refers to gluttony in the same breath with drunkenness, as if they were the same sin simply with different substances (Prov. 23:20; 28:7 NASB). In Titus 1:12 Paul lists being a glutton alongside other sins, such as lying and evil behavior worthy of rebuke.

The Bible clearly teaches that God did not give us food so that we could abuse it or use it as a substitute for dealing with issues that should be brought to him for processing and resolution. Food can easily become for us an idol that we give homage to or a habit that controls us and robs us of our health and leadership effectiveness. Exercising physical self-leadership will mean that we give sustained attention to the component of diet and nutrition.

Weight Management

Another component that is closely related to diet and nutrition is personal weight management. As mentioned previously, the weight problem in America has reached acute status at the beginning of the twenty-first century. More than at any time in history, a large percentage of our population is overweight to the point of being considered clinically obese. Certainly this is not a condition that causes God to be glorified in our body.

Now, to be honest, I decided to include this section with some fear and trepidation. I in no way want this encouragement toward healthy weight management to be construed as license to become obsessed with our weight and appearance. It is as easy to err on the side of obsessing about our body and its weight as it is to ignore and abuse our body in this area. Again, as with everything in the Christian life, balance is the key.

First of all, let me establish what I am not advocating. I am not suggesting or encouraging that we strive for the perfect body. The weight management component of physical self-leadership is not primarily about appearance or aesthetics, it is about maintaining a weight that will promote our healthy and physical longevity barring unforeseen illness or accident. This requires that we understand the body type that God has given us and the genes that we have inherited from our family of origin. What may be a healthy weight for us could very well be unhealthy for another person. We must work with what God has given us and learn to be content with it. This also means that what was a healthy weight for us at twenty may not be realistic at forty. But again, such variables are not to be used as excuses for poor or nonexistent weight management.

Being grossly overweight and addicted to food is one of the few addictions and spiritual problems that we merely wink at in Christian circles, but it should not be so. If, as the Scripture teaches, we are to glorify God with our physical body, then maintaining the proper weight for our body is essential. There are few things that reflect a lack of self-leadership and self-control (a fruit of the Holy Spirit, by the way) than a Christian leader who is suffering from a severe case of "Dunlaps Disease" (where a person's midsection overlaps his belt to the point that the belt disappears). Few things will so publicly report our struggle with gluttony than will a significantly overweight body.

I am well aware that I have likely offended some readers sufficiently at this point that they are ready to write the publisher for a refund; but let me assure you that is not my intention. I firmly believe that this is a vital area of self-leadership that must not be overlooked.

Also, I realize that some people have difficulty controlling their weight because of some chronic illness or immobility. Yet, at the same time, they are called to be conscious of what they eat and to take care of their body to the extent that they can. We all know whether our weight problem is due to illness or due to poor self-leadership. Wise and effective leaders will take seriously this component of self-leadership.

Physical Fitness

The third component of physical self-leadership involves our level of physical fitness. As you have probably noticed by this time, all of these components are closely related to one another and, in fact, can't help but impact each other. If we eat poorly it will impact our weight, which will in turn impact our level of fitness, which will then more than likely impact the way we feel about ourselves and possibly even become a drain on our spiritual vitality.

The way that we exercise self-leadership over this component of our physical life is through exercise and activity. God created our bodies to move and be active, not sedentary. Suffice it to say that exercise should be a regular, nonnegotiable part of any leader's weekly schedule. Exercise is as important to us as any other aspect of our leadership and one to which we must attend.

Because this is not a book on exercise and fitness I am not going to suggest any physical routines for you. I will say that if you are not exercising regularly at the present time, you must begin now. Don't wait until it is convenient or until you feel like it because that time will never come.

I have realized the importance of physical fitness and have tried to be faithful to a routine of regular exercise over the last twenty years. My morning routine is so predictable that I am sure it would bore must people to death, but for me it is a daily adventure that I greatly look forward to most days. I rise to my alarm at 5:15 and immediately make my morning coffee. While the coffee is brewing I scan the morning paper, noticing important stories and clipping anything that might be useful to me in a future writing project or sermon series. Once my coffee is ready, I move downstairs to my study and begin my spiritual disciplines—this lasts until about 7:00 A.M. At 7:00 I dress for my morning workout. I pull out the Nordic Track that I have been using for the past five years and ski over figurative hill and dale as I watch the morning news programs. My session on the Nordic Track lasts until about 7:45 A.M. at which time I pull out my Total Gym and engage in a fifteen- to twenty-minute strength workout. Once this is complete I stretch and prepare for my shower. Almost without exception, I am in the office by 9:30 and ready to engage in the day's activities feeling fresh and with an abundance of energy. I follow this routine four days a week, Monday through Thursday, with a slight variation on Friday, which is my day off.

On several days during the week I often jump on the Nordic Track for an evening workout.

Now obviously this is not appropriate for anyone except me. We are all different. But I share it only to suggest that we all need some type of routine when it comes to exercise or else it will never get done. The reason I like to do it in the morning is because I enjoy the balance of completing my spiritual disciplines and physical disciplines in the same time period. I engage in personal soul care and then I engage in some physical resource management. They just seem to fit together this way and, for me, are more meaningful.

Personal Medical Care

Finally, it is absolutely vital that we take responsibility for our personal medical care. And when we cross that magic threshold into middle age, it becomes even more vital to engage in proactive personal medical care.

Just before beginning this chapter, I scheduled what my physician calls a 50,000-mile checkup. Now that I am forty-one, I feel it is important to begin receiving annual physicals just to make sure that everything is still in the right place and that all of my parts are in good working order as they should be. Unfortunately we hesitate to have regular physicals because, ridiculous as it sounds, we are afraid the doctor may find something wrong! If we truly are worried that the doctor may find something wrong, isn't that exactly the place we should go? Denial and fear never promote good health nor will they prevent serious illness; they can only contribute to poor health. For a list of helpful Web sites that address health and exercise issues, see appendix B.

PERSONAL REST AND RECREATION

Another element of physical self-leadership that complements our personal resource management involves the vital role personal recreation plays in our overall leadership effectiveness.

A few years ago the president of Harvard University, Neil Rudenstine, crashed and burned emotionally and physically in the middle of a major fund-raising campaign for the university.

It began the day the normally hard-driving, early-to-rise Rudenstine overslept and had difficulty getting out of bed. The Ivy League president was unceremoniously confronted and overcome by his own emotional and physical exhaustion. After years of running his leadership engine in high gear, it was finally beginning to seize up.

His doctor prescribed a sabbatical—an extended Sabbath—during which time he could allow his body, mind, and emotions to recover and be refreshed. President Rudenstine complied and took an extended break. During his time away, he read essayist Lewis Thomas, listened to the music of Ravel, and took long, relaxing walks on the beach with his wife. After three months of long overdue refreshment and restoration, he was able to resume his duties, but he returned to work with an understanding of the vital role the Sabbath principle plays in the life of a healthy leader.

The week after he returned to his post, his picture graced the cover of *Newsweek* magazine under the headline "Exhausted!" The feature story focused on the importance of top-level leaders' making personal rest and restoration a high priority in their crowded schedule if they desire to keep leading well.[4]

Today we are people desperately in need of rest and recreation that is genuinely restorative and renewing. Unfortunately, however, as with many other concepts, our frenetic twenty-first-century American culture has distorted and compromised the concept of recreation. All too often the forms of recreation in which many leaders engage today actually contribute to their feelings of frustration and stress rather than reduce them.

One of the most common forms of recreation for many people involves watching some sporting event on television or attending an event in person. Other frequent recreational pursuits include fast-paced, high-cost vacations to exotic places, going out to eat, going to the movies, spending the weekend at one or more of the numerous amusement parks located in almost every region of the country, or wandering around at the local mall, which for many people has become a low-cost form of recreation.

None of these activities fit the classic definition of recreation. Today we equate recreation with entertainment or amusing ourselves. For many leaders, recreation has become a way of simply being distracted or diverted from the responsibilities and pressures of a fast-paced, driven life. But that is not the purpose of true recreation.

The word *recreation* has as its root meaning, "to refresh." It refers to any play or activity that relaxes and refreshes the body or mind. True recreation has as its intended purpose the restoration of a person's body and spirit to full health. Similarly, the word *vacation* means a period of time free from work or study. A vacation is to be taken for the purpose of creating some vacant space in our normally overcrowded and frenzied life.

True recreation involves strategically engaging in activities and pursuits that will enable us to experience a measure of emotional, spiritual, and physical restoration. To engage in genuine recreation is to experience a measure of "re-creation." It should serve the purpose of helping us once again find a place of balance and center in our lives. It should provide time for us to think deeply and creatively about our life and what is really important to us as well as how we are living out our values as we move toward the fulfillment of our life goals. Times of genuine recreation provide us with valuable time and space to evaluate our life with a perspective that is not possible in the midst of our normal daily routine. We will know when we have engaged in genuine recreation because we will feel refreshed and restored; we will have a renewed sense of our Calling and new stores of energy and enthusiasm to continue our leadership journey.

All of the activities I mentioned earlier, like watching television, going on high-cost, rigidly scheduled vacations, visiting amusement parks, and other similar activities, often leave us feeling anything but refreshed and restored. It is easy to return from such experiences feeling even worse than before. It is virtually impossible to regain our balance and find renewed energy to pursue our Calling while watching a fast-paced sporting event. Seldom will we experience spiritual or physical restoration while waiting in endless lines and madly dashing about the overcrowded grounds of an amusement park, all the while listening to our children beg for yet one more cheap trinket. That is not to say that there is anything wrong with these activities; it is just that they are better suited to entertainment and merriment, not recreation.

So what would qualify as recreation? I suggest following at least one rule of thumb when planning a period of recreation: the simpler the better. Here are a few examples:

For several summers, our family has rented a small cabin in the north woods of Wisconsin. The cabin has no television, no radio, and I have to drive nearly twenty miles to pick up a copy of any newspaper. We spend our days lounging in front of the lake reading books, playing games with our children, taking long nature hikes, and just napping under the pines with nothing but the chirping of the birds and the sound of the lake lapping at the shore to ease us into slumberland. In the evenings, we sit around the campfire, tell stories, and read out loud to one another. By the end of just one week in this setting I feel as if I've been gone for a month. I feel refreshed and renewed and ready to return to my church with a new perspective and enthusiasm.

Just about every other year I spend a week fly-fishing on the Green River in northeast Utah with a close Christian friend who is also the leader of a high-stress, fast-paced organization. We have no schedule. There are no appointments. There is no artificial noise—just the sounds of nature. We engage in nightly fireside conversations in which we discuss philosophy, theology, our dreams and goals, the present state of our spiritual journey, and many other diverse subjects. At other times, we just sit and gaze into the vast expanse of the universe that fills our view from horizon to horizon with the brilliant spectacle of countless heavenly bodies, stunned into silence by the realization of God's greatness and our place in his creation. I have never completed one of these trips without experiencing a profound sense of renewal and balance.

This summer I am going to be hiking the entire 100-mile length of the Centennial Trail in the Black Hills of South Dakota with my thirteen-year-old son, Seth. Along the way, we will journal our experiences and talk a lot. We will learn new things about one another, God's creation, and ourselves. We will deepen our relationship with days of uninterrupted time together. And I know we will both come home refreshed and restored: I to my pastoral leadership duties, and Seth to the challenges of the seventh grade and blossoming adolescence.

There are as many different ways to engage in genuine recreation as there are people and personalities. It is up to each of us to find the forms of recreation that work best for us. For some it may be vacations spent painting or drawing. Others may find restoration and renewal exploring some new land and learning a new culture. Still others will find renewal going to their lake cottage to engage in gardening or bird watching. We can even take brief recreation breaks that don't require travel. We can spend an evening quietly reading to the soothing sound of good music. For me an evening spent tying flies for some future trip can be a brief form of restoration. Needlepoint, writing poetry, taking a walk, going for a bike ride, or lying in the grass in our own backyard can all be simple forms of recreation—mini-vacations, if you will. What we do is not nearly as important as what it produces within us. A vital element of physical self-leadership is taking the time to engage in true recreation that brings physical, spiritual, and emotional renewal.

Obstacles to Effective Physical Self-Leadership

As with any attempts to exercise strong leadership and bring transformation to existing paradigms, whether organizationally or personally, we will inevitably face forces that will conspire against our best efforts and encounter obstacles that will keep us from realizing the transformation we desire. It is important that we identify these potential obstacles and plan ways to overcome them before we encounter them.

TELEVISION

I firmly believe that television is one of the most powerful forces that will prevent us from exercising effective physical self-leadership. We are a society that has become literally addicted to television. If you don't believe me, just decide to go without for even one month—I mean cold turkey, no television whatsoever! Most of us feel as if we can't live without it, though we could receive the same information via the radio, news magazines, or the daily newspaper.

This addiction to television has created one of the most sedentary populations in the history of the world. We have been reduced to living our lives vicariously through television characters and televised adventures. Rather than living the adventures ourselves, we have become sadly content to watch others live them.

Television has become the Christian drug of choice right next to food. When we are bored or stressed or down or in need of genuine recreation, we turn on the tube and sit there for hours on end, our brains completely disengaged from any critical thought or reflection that might bring the renewal we seek.

Often one of our favorite activities as we scan the channels is eating. We eat not out of hunger or the desire to fuel our body but because we are so incredibly bored! We need to realize that any time spent watching television is time that cannot be given to exercise, recreation, or any other productive endeavor. That is not to say that television offers nothing of value. There are interesting and informative profiles of leaders, programs that provide analysis of current events, and even education offerings that can be beneficial. Still, if we are ever going to engage in the ongoing exercise of effective physical self-leadership, it will almost invariably require that we overcome the television-induced inertia that a vast majority of the American public suffers. Mark this well—there will be many times when you could be doing something productive for your body and you will opt instead to mindlessly "veg out" in front of the plug-in drug. Be prepared to fight the battle.

LACK OF A PLAN

The second major obstacle to growth in the area of physical self-leadership is the lack of any concrete plan. Without a plan we will almost always falter, regardless of what it is we attempt.

It is important that you take the time and energy to assess your current condition and then develop a written plan that can serve as a daily guide as you seek to address the various issues of physical self-leadership. How much weight do you need to lose? How many points do you need to reduce your cholesterol and how specifically do you plan to do that? What exercises will you engage in and how often will you do so? When and how will you engage in recreation and what will it consist of? These are all questions that should be answered in your plan. As the hackneyed saying goes, "Failing to plan is planning to fail." Nowhere is that more true than in the exercise of physical self-leadership.

PROCRASTINATION

The final obstacle that we have to battle is procrastination. The tendency to put off until tomorrow what can and should be done today is a universal and constant obstacle to just about everything we will ever want to achieve in life. "I'll begin my exercise program after the New Year." "I will begin regular recreation as soon as this project is complete or this busy season passes." "Once I get in shape, then I'll schedule a doctor's appointment." "As soon as I can afford to join the health club, I'll begin to exercise" All of these well-intentioned statements are the product of procrastination.

As I mentioned in the chapter on motivation (chapter 5), knowing what to do and doing what we know are two entirely different matters. The difference between simply knowing and doing is finding the motivation necessary. Moving through procrastination to implement what we know makes a tangible and positive contribution to both our life and the effective exercise of our leadership.

A SELF-LEADERSHIP WORKSHOP

1. Which of your life values fall most noticeably into the venue of physical self-leadership? Review your personal constitution, following chapter 5, and list your physical self-leadership values

here. If you do not have any values that apply to your physical life, now is the time to go back to the drawing board and develop one or two. With no physical values, your life is significantly out of balance and your attempts at effective, wholistic self-leadership are diminished.

My Physical Self-Leadership Values

-

-

-

-

-

-

2. Which of the Elements of Physical Self-Leadership would most enable you to move consistently in the direction of this/these values?

Physical Resource Management

Diet & Nutrition

Physical Fitness

Weight Management

Personal Medical Care

Personal Rest and Recreation

In the grid that follows, list the two *most* important elements and then the two that are of *secondary* importance to you at the present time:

173

Top Two	
Second Two	

Now, develop a plan to begin leading yourself in the top two elements listed above. Be specific about how you plan to incorporate these into your practice of self-leadership.

Element of Physical Self-Leadership	Action to Take

3. Identify the one obstacle to effective physical self-leadership that will sabotage your efforts.

Obstacle	How and why it will block my efforts in physical self-leadership

4. Now write three concrete actions you will take to overcome this obstacle.

Obstacle	Actions to Overcome Obstacle

8

EMOTIONAL SELF-LEADERSHIP

MASTERING OUR MOODS

During the early months of 1972, the presidential campaign to determine who would occupy the White House was just beginning to take shape. President Nixon was busy denying and defending himself from allegations related to the break-in at the Watergate complex. Inflation was rampant. The Vietnam War was still droning on in spite of the president's promises to bring the troops home. And the American people seemed ready for a change in the political scenery in the nation's capital.

It was into this chaotic political milieu that a promising new candidate for the highest office in the land eagerly thrust himself. Edmund S. Muskie was a Democratic senator from the state of Maine and, by all accounts, a brilliant politician who also possessed a shining intellect. In no time and with very little effort or formal organization, Muskie became the widely acknowledged front-runner for the Democratic nomination.

However, big-time politics are not for the fainthearted or the thin-skinned. As they are now, personal attacks and vicious rumors were the accepted coin of the realm for presidential politics. Once Muskie's status as front-runner became generally accepted, he was subjected to a barrage of personal attacks and slurs. In fact President Nixon's reelection committee, known as CREEP (Committee to Reelect the President), made the Maine senator a special target of its hardball tactics, doing anything and everything it could to embarrass and humiliate the newly christened top contender.

Clearly these attacks were beginning to take their emotional toll on the presidential hopeful. But when one aspires to be the leader of the free world, overcoming such tactics and maintaining control of one's emotions are essential prerequisites.

As he was campaigning in New Hampshire, an important state for the senator to do well in, Muskie made one appearance that wrote the end of the story for his presidential aspirations. Under the weight of the personal attacks he was being subjected to, Senator Muskie broke down and cried under the emotional pressure. The embarrassing episode was caught on film and replayed over and over again across the nation's airwaves and splashed on the front page of virtually every newspaper in the country. It was to be an emotional eruption from which he would never fully recover politically.

Senator Edmund Muskie was a brilliant man, a skilled politician, a seasoned leader, and the acknowledged front-runner for his party's nomination, but his inability to control his emotions during one public appearance proved to be extremely costly and ultimately prevented him from exercising his leadership on a much broader scale.

During the 1999 Wimbledon Tennis Championship, Martina Hingis learned the hard way how her moods could do to her what few world-class tennis players could. Though she was ranked the number one female tennis player in the world and was seeded number one in the tournament, she was soundly beaten in her first match by a previously unknown young player.

In the worst upset in Wimbledon history, Martina Hingis was thrashed 6-2, 6-0, in just fifty-five minutes. In spite of her considerable skill, experience, and the intimidation factor of being ranked number one in the world, she was humiliated by a sixteen-year-old rookie.

The reason for the beating was attributed to emotions and moods. Before her match Martina had had an argument with her mother, resulting in her mother's leaving the tournament. In an emotionally fragile state, Martina could not perform at her normal level of excellence—she was beaten before she ever set foot on the luscious grass court at Wimbledon. The reality is that Martina Hingis was not beaten by another player, she was defeated by her moods.

THE MENACE OF MOODS

A gifted young pastor who was a colleague of mine had sterling personal character, an exceptional education, a passion for Christ and his church, and unlimited potential. One of the only limitations to his future ministry effectiveness was his dark moods, which would periodically overcome him, often at the most awkward and public of times.

On more than one occasion, this pastor would come to a meeting with lay people, his angry mood written across his face and emotional venom seeping out with every word he spoke. It wasn't that he was upset with anyone in the meeting; he was simply being overcome by a foul mood that had its genesis in a previous episode or encounter. It wasn't long before these foul moods began to hinder the effectiveness of his ministry. On several occasions parishioners came to me as the senior pastor wanting to know what was wrong with this pastor. His inability to master his moods was quickly becoming the topic of congregational discussion.

Fortunately this young pastor became aware of the ramifications of his problem and began to take proactive steps to learn how he could overcome his dour moods before they began to erode his credibility and hinder his leadership effectiveness. Today this leader has a bright future. Not that he never struggles with oppressive moods—all leaders have to confront menacing moods from time to time—it's just that now he is better able to sense

179

their onset and exercise the necessary self-leadership to keep them from bleeding into his public ministry. But not all leaders learn how to master their moods before they have a negative and debilitating effect.

It is possible to have mastered virtually every area of self-leadership and be a leader of unquestioned integrity and still have one's leadership effectiveness undermined by an inability to control and overcome negative, destructive moods. The reality is that the way we either control or fail to control this important area of our life has a profound impact on how productively we will exercise our Calling, flesh out our values, and realize our life goals. Additionally, few things in life can sap us of our motivation and desires like being whipped around by errant and uneven emotions.

As we will see, senators, tennis champions, and rookie pastors are not the only ones who have had to struggle with the painful consequences that come as a result of failing to exercise self-leadership over their emotions. Throughout history we read of leaders who failed in leadership or had their leadership cut short as a result of their menacing and uncontrolled moods. Even biblical leaders of great influence and renown suffered serious and often substantial consequences as a result of failing to exercise leadership over this area of their life.

The Bible is full of leaders who were called and gifted by God, experienced significant victories, and still suffered the consequences of uncontrolled emotions.

ABRAHAM

We are familiar with the story of how Abraham heeded God's call to leave Ur and by faith left his home and family for a strange land. Throughout his long life Abraham exhibited great faith and a supernatural trust in God, yet there were times when his emotions got the best of him and came close to jeopardizing his usefulness as God's chosen leader.

In Genesis 12:10–20 we read of Abraham's encounter with fear as he entered the land of Egypt with his beautiful wife, Sarah. Abraham was so overcome with the fear that he might be killed because of Sarah's beauty that he concocted an unfortunate lie to protect himself, though he clearly put his wife and God's plan in jeopardy.

Later in his life, Abraham again lost an important battle with his emotions. After God promised to give Abraham a son by his wife, Sarah, Abraham grew impatient with the time God was taking to fulfill the promise and so, no doubt fueled by his impatience, he decided to take control of the situation by impregnating his wife's handmaiden, Hagar (Gen. 16:1–16). The result of this emotionally induced lapse in faith produced Abraham's son, Ishmael, and a future of turmoil and trouble that cast a long shadow over the eventual fulfillment of God's promise in the birth of Sarah's child, Isaac. It can safely be said that the current turmoil we now experience in the world between the Jews and Palestinians is a direct result of Abraham's inability to master his impatience and frustration—a momentary mood with historic consequences.

MOSES

One of the more troubling and certainly sobering emotional episodes involving a biblical leader is Moses' eruption at Meribah as recorded in Numbers 20.

God had commanded Moses to provide water for the people of Israel by issuing a command to a rock. Had Moses obeyed, God would have produced an amazing miracle on the basis of a simple verbal command. Instead, Moses allowed himself to be overcome by his emotions. For months prior to this occasion the people had been whining and complaining about their hardships in the wilderness since being liberated from their Egyptian captivity. In spite of Moses' provision and care for the people, they had been continually chafing against his leadership. Finally, all of the complaints and pettiness had taken their toll on Moses.

Rather than simply commanding the rock to produce water for his weary charges, Moses let his anger and frustration with the people bleed into his public exercise of leadership on God's behalf. He gathered the people around the rock and sarcastically called them a bunch of rebels. Then, in a fit of frustration that resulted from the people constantly expecting him to do the

181

impossible, Moses yelled at the people, "Listen, you rebels, shall we bring water for you out of this rock?" Next, with what I am sure had to have been a great measure of satisfaction, he struck the rock with his staff and water came gushing out to satisfy the people's thirst. But God was not pleased with his leader. In response to Moses' emotional eruption that led to this disobedience God said, "Because you did not trust me enough to demonstrate my holiness to the people of Israel, you will not lead them into the land I am giving them" (v. 12).

Moses was not allowed to lead the people into the promised land because of a humiliating bout with uncontrolled emotions that revealed he did not trust God to deal with the rebellious people and reward his faithfulness accordingly. I believe God's surprisingly harsh discipline in the case of Moses also had to do with how his public outburst of anger and frustration probably discredited him in the eyes of the people and certainly in the eyes of God. My guess is that if Moses had emoted in private with a trusted advisor or recorded his frustration in a journal—as King David was apparently in the habit of doing—there would have been no consequences at all. It wasn't the feelings of frustration and anger Moses felt that God was punishing, but rather his inability or unwillingness to maintain control over them while engaged in public leadership.

Elijah

Another leader who struggled with menacing moods and wild emotions was the great prophet Elijah. In 1 Kings, Scripture records the incredible things that God did through this leader. In chapter 17, Elijah is used by God to bring a severe drought on the land for three years. Immediately on the heels of this pronouncement, Elijah is used by God to bring a widow's dead son back to life. Then in chapter 18, Elijah confronts the prophets of Baal and is used to demonstrate the power and presence of God by calling fire down from heaven to consume a waterlogged sacrifice. Shortly thereafter, Elijah demonstrated God's power to King Ahab by calling an end to the punishing drought.

But then in chapter 19, the story of Elijah takes an unexpected turn. Elijah seems to have an emotional breakdown of sorts. He is suddenly overcome with fear, discouragement, and suicidal depression. This emotional onslaught was no doubt at least partially the result of an incredibly dramatic and stressful period of what appears to be nonstop, high-profile ministry. Another factor that contributed to his sudden emotional paralysis was the death threat he received from Queen Jezebel. But whatever its ultimate cause, Elijah's fear, discouragement, and depression caused him to tuck his tail and run for his life!

Here is a leader who had been used by God to raise the dead, declare a three-year drought, defeat the assembled prophets of Baal, and call rain down from heaven to end the drought, yet was so overcome by his emotions that he was completely debilitated.

Unquestionably, emotions can become a friend or foe depending on whether or not they can be controlled to some degree by the leader experiencing them. We should not strive to eliminate our emotions by suppressing them, but we must also not allow our emotions to become so acute that they overwhelm and debilitate us, as was the case in Elijah's life. Emotional self-leadership means that we will maintain emotional balance. Failure to exercise effective self-leadership over our emotions and allowing them to control us can greatly hinder our usefulness and effectiveness in whatever leadership role God has placed us. If God did not hesitate to discipline Moses for his emotional outburst, and if God allowed the result of Abraham's emotional lapse to remain with us until this day, it would seem presumptuous for us to assume that we are somehow exempt from the negative consequences that can result from failing to master our moods.

THE BIBLE AND OUR EMOTIONS

When it comes to the exercise of leadership, there are some emotions that are more menacing than others. The emotions of anger, fear, worry, and depression are among the most difficult to control and, consequently, can cause the greatest trouble when a leader fails to exercise the appropriate control over them in the exercise of public leadership.

ANGER

Few human emotions can be as powerful and destructive as anger. I personally know many leaders who have allowed anger to get the best of them in a public setting or while interacting with those to whom they gave leadership, only to have their outburst erode their credibility and ultimately undermine their leadership. Countless pastors have left churches, and even the ministry altogether, ultimately as a result of being unable to control their anger. Anger that has not been appropriately processed will never lead to any constructive or positive action. Anger blurs our vision and distorts our perspective. When we allow our exercise of leadership to be influenced or controlled by unprocessed anger, there will always be detrimental consequences.

In Psalm 37, David advises, "Stop your anger! Turn from your rage! Do not envy others—it only leads to harm" (v. 8). In Proverbs David's son Solomon dispenses this wisdom regarding anger: "A hot-tempered person starts fights and gets into all kinds of sin" (Prov. 29:22). Again Solomon speaks about the wisdom of learning to control one's anger when he writes, "People with good sense restrain their anger; they earn esteem by overlooking wrongs" (19:11). While public eruptions of anger erode a leader's credibility and esteem in the eyes of those he or she leads, the ability to restrain one's anger, and when appropriate even overlook certain offenses, causes a leader to be more highly esteemed and respected for his or her emotional steadiness, particularly when under the pressure of personal attacks and criticism.

Other proverbs also speak to the importance of controlling our anger. Proverbs 19:19 says, "Short-tempered people must pay their own penalty"; and Proverbs 20:3 advises, "Avoiding a fight is a mark of honor; only fools insist on quarreling." Even more dramatic is the counsel given in Proverbs 22:24–25 regarding the need to avoid anger: "Keep away from angry, short-tempered people, or you will learn to be like them and endanger your soul." In a similar tone, the apostle Paul speaks of the spiritual danger we open ourselves up to when we fail to master our anger. "And 'don't sin by letting anger gain control over you.' Don't let the sun go down while you are still angry, for anger gives a mighty foothold to the Devil" (Eph. 4:26–27).

Abraham Lincoln was often the subject of personal attacks and heated criticism as he led our divided and warring nation through the tumult of the Civil War. There were times when Lincoln would seethe with anger in response to the harsh, unfair attacks of his opponents and critics. But President Lincoln had also learned the importance of restraining his anger. When he could contain his anger no longer, he would sit down and write a letter addressed to the person who had kindled his anger. He would allow his anger and feelings of hurt to spill unedited onto the page. Then, once he finished composing the cathartic epistle, he would carry it in the breast pocket of his coat until he had fully processed his anger, then he would destroy the letter. It was a tool he used often to master this destructive emotion, enabling him to lead with dignity and stability during an extremely chaotic period of history when the emotions of the rest of the country were often uncontrolled.

Unfortunately, in contrast to Lincoln, many other leaders have had to learn the hard way the costly lessons that often result from uncontrolled anger. In American leadership circles Senator John McCain came under fire for his legendary hot temper. Many in the media and even his opponents in the presidential election of 2000 queried whether he was fit to lead because of his periodic battles with unrestrained anger.

Even within the ranks of Christian leadership the inability to control angry outbursts has cost more than one leader his or her position. In the October 25, 1999, issue of *Christianity Today* it was reported that Mark T. Coppenger was dismissed as president of Midwestern Baptist Theological Seminary, stating that his "expressions of anger" had "irreparably damaged his ability to lead [the] seminary."[1]

If we have clearly articulated our values and connected with our Calling, few things will enable us to flesh out our Calling before the people we lead quite like learning to maintain a measure of emotional stability, particularly during those difficult times when others with less control allow their raw, random emotions to contribute to the chaos.

FEAR AND WORRY

In his book, *The Culture of Fear,* author Barry Glassner makes the case that Americans are seemingly afraid of everything.[2] According to Glassner, our American culture thrives on the constant creation of issues and plagues that we should worry about and fear. Politicians attempt to lure voters with the promise that their policies and programs will protect constituents from all of the things of which they are afraid. And, if the voters are not already sufficiently afraid of the current state of affairs, you can count on these political aspirants, ably assisted by the news media, to create some fear by their use of dire statistics, gloomy prognostications, and sensational stories.

It seems that today people are fearful of a whole litany of cultural, political, economic, educational, and even scientific maladies. Fears abound regarding things such as crime, drugs, AIDS, teenage violence, economic recession, pollution, global warming, air disasters, racial unrest, corrupt leaders, the possible collapse of the health care system, natural disasters, organized crime, gambling, road rage, and the list could go on endlessly.

These fears and worries are cultivated and perpetuated by a media that seems intent on breaking the next big story that will grip the airwaves for months at a time. The American viewing public is constantly served up a menu of fear-mongering stories about such things as unsanitary food handling in restaurants, abusive child care providers, corrupt telemarketers, violence in schools, incompetent physicians and pharmacists, and countless other worry-inducing pieces delivered by an army of undercover journalists.

After the tragedy in the spring of 1999 at Columbine High School in Littleton, Colorado, in which fourteen students and one teacher were killed, the Fox News Network dedicated weeks to every possible angle of the story under the ever-present headline and artist's graphic "Terror in the Rockies!" Of course the

Fox network was not alone. The media was in a feeding frenzy as they covered the story, making it seem like the latest made-for-TV miniseries.

Rather than simply reporting the story, the various media outlets did everything possible to exacerbate the fears of the public by rehearsing ad nauseam the accounts of eye witnesses, the reflections of experts, the commentary of cultural pundits, and the posturing of politicians.

Though, admittedly, all is not perfect in America, and we have without question experienced a negative slide in our moral values during the past fifty years, living in fear and obsessively worrying about everything that can possibly go wrong is not a productive approach—particularly not for Christians and Christian leaders.

As spiritual leaders, we must not be among those who use fear to rally the troops. Rather, we are to be modern-day prophets, heralding a message of hope that will promote an unshakable confidence in Jesus Christ and the promises of Scripture. When we as leaders allow ourselves to be seduced by our current culture of fear, we become part of the problem rather than positive promoters of the solutions.

Nothing should be more uncharacteristic of Christians than fear. The apostle Paul wrote to his young protégé Timothy during an incredible period of cultural upheaval. Christians were being imprisoned and executed for their faith in Christ, and Jewish converts were being ostracized from their communities and subjected to persecution. Paul himself knew his life was in jeopardy because of the message he was propagating. And yet, in spite of the fact that Paul had every reason to be fearful and to melodramatically warn Timothy, he chose to write, "For God has not given us a spirit of fear and timidity, but of power, love, and self-discipline" (2 Tim. 1:7). Exhorting Timothy to not curtail his proclamation of the Christian gospel because of the likelihood of reprisals, Paul urges him to exercise self-discipline over his fear and keep doing the work to which he had been called.

King David was a man who knew what it was like to be in extremely dangerous, life-threatening situations. He had more reasons than most of us today to be gripped with fear-induced pessimism. And yet in Psalm 56:3–4 he wrote, "When I am afraid, I put my trust in you. O God, I praise your word. I trust in God, so why should I be afraid? What can mere mortals do to me?"

David understood that when we choose to focus on all of the turmoil and troubles of this world to the extent that they create within us fear and obsessive worry, it is a clear indication that we are no longer trusting in God. Whether our fear is fueled by crime, drugs, the AIDS epidemic, the uncertainties of the stock market and the economy, pollution, or any other social malady, we must realize, as those who have placed our faith in a sovereign God, that we have nothing to fear. God is in control even when it appears that the world is in the grip of chaotic entropy and is hurtling toward destruction.

When the nation of Israel was experiencing a time of fearful chaos that did in fact result in a period of national uncertainty and temporary removal from their land, God spoke through the prophet Isaiah saying, "Don't be afraid, for I am with you. Do not be dismayed, for I am your God. I will strengthen you. I will help you. I will uphold you with my victorious right hand" (Isa. 41:10). Even when the world seemed to be at its worst, God's promise was that he was in control and would continue to protect them—they would ultimately be victorious over their chaotic circumstances.

It is imperative, particularly in a social climate so permeated by fear, that we leaders not allow ourselves to be overcome by fear and worry. We must constantly lead our lives with an unwavering confidence that our God is in absolute sovereign control of all things.

As Christian leaders, we have something to offer the world that politicians and government policies alone cannot deliver. We can offer those we lead a transcendent hope for the future that is not based on human effort and ingenuity, but rather on a relationship with the sovereign God of the cosmos who has already determined the ultimate end of human history and is actively engaged in superintending every event toward the fulfillment of that predetermined plan.

It is with that kind of hope in mind that the apostle Paul was able to say from a Roman prison cell where he awaited his own execution:

Don't worry about anything; instead, pray about everything. Tell God what you need, and thank him for all he has done. If you do this you will experience God's peace, which is far more wonderful than the human mind can understand. His peace will guard your hearts and minds as you live in Christ Jesus.

Philippians 4:6–7

The key is that we can overcome fear and worry as we consciously live our lives in relationship with Jesus Christ, the Creator and Sustainer of every atom that comprises every piece of matter in the universe and beyond.

We cannot expect to provide strong leadership if our self-leadership is so ineffective that we are unable to overcome our own fears and worries. How easily we can find ourselves driven by irrational fears and worries to take unhealthy and unwise action! For those who provide leadership to churches and other nonprofit organizations, it is easy to become gripped by fears of plummeting giving or organizational decline. Pastors can worry about key families leaving the church and unhappy members undermining their leadership. It is easy to become overwhelmed with fear and worry when confronted with a multimillion-dollar building project and all of the what if's that accompany such efforts. When people don't like us or when we think our preaching is not all that it should be, we may begin to disintegrate emotionally under the pressure. That is why we must give strong leadership to this area of our lives and place our hope and trust in the One who has called and entrusted us with leadership on his behalf. If we fail to get a handle on our fear and worry, it will ultimately lead to a state of melancholy and depression that will threaten our ability to lead.

Depression

The great British preacher Charles Haddon Spurgeon was a man of immense talent and intense emotion. In fact Spurgeon, one of the most prominent pastors of his era, spent many of his years overcome by life-threatening bouts of depression and melancholy. In his classic book referenced earlier, *Lectures to My*

Students, the great preacher confessed his struggle with dark moods when he wrote, "Knowing by most painful experience what deep depression of spirit means, being visited therewith at seasons by no means few or far between."[3]

I must confess that when I first read those words as a young pastor struggling through the ups and downs of an extremely demanding and difficult church experience, it was as if they had been written directly to me. For several years I had found myself doing periodic battle with what I could only describe then as dark spells. For no reason whatsoever, often during times of great success and accomplishment, I would find myself suddenly immobilized by a sense of foreboding and hopelessness. This would lead to extended stays in my locked study with the lights off, listening to music that echoed my inner mood. These episodes could come at any time and with no warning at all, often lasting for a month at a time. Over time I found these periods of darkness coming with more regularity and increasing severity. Finally, it became clear that I would not be able to provide effective leadership while slogging through my own depression, and I sought the expertise of a psychiatrist who could help me make sense of what was happening to me.

Over a period of years, I began to learn what was happening in my life and how I could find lasting relief from this frightening nemesis of depression. I am happy to say that today I am no longer plagued by such periods of darkness. Though, like everyone, I endure those times when I am emotionally down or sad, I no longer endure episodes of melancholy so acute that they drive me to the darkness of a locked study.

For me, exercising self-leadership in this area is an ongoing effort. It has required me to learn about myself and how I am wired, as well as special techniques, lifestyle practices, and patterns of thought that enable me to maintain an acceptable and enjoyable balance over my emotional states.

Never before have there been more demands and pressures for those in positions of spiritual leadership. As a result of these increased demands and expectations, a higher percentage of pastors than ever before are leaving the ministry as a result of burnout and depression. In an ecclesiastical culture that expects pastors to build "seven-day-a-week" churches on resources that can scarcely maintain weekend programs, and create ministries to attract a populace that now demands church programs that can compete with the entertainment industry, many pastors are buckling under the unrealistic expectations.

In the June 14, 1999, issue of *Newsweek* magazine, the cover was dedicated to the increasingly serious issue of stress. The headline on the cover read, "STRESS: How it attacks your body." The articles inside the magazine proceeded to explain how devastating and debilitating stress can be when we fail to understand it and take the necessary steps to deal therapeutically with this modern-day menace.

An article titled "Ministers under Stress" that appeared in the April 14, 1991, issue of *Parade* magazine documented the effects of stress on spiritual leaders:

> Public scandals involving over stressed clergy often result from sexual misconduct with parishioners—"carnaling out," as ministers refer to it—but prolonged stress is also a factor in alcoholism, drug abuse, overeating and other addictions. It can mean depression, anxiety, heart attacks or cancer.[4]

In an effort to provide relief and balance for emotionally crushed clergy, many denominations are providing regular counseling and therapy services for their ministers. My own denomination, the Baptist General Conference, regularly provides getaways called "RevivUs Summits" for pastoral couples who are seriously struggling with burnout, depression, and other debilitating emotional problems. In just the last several years this program has been utilized by eighty-two clergy couples.

For those who have experienced it, however, trying to effectively minister while caught in the depths of depression and the inner darkness and crushed spirit it spawns is virtually impossible. Perhaps as a result of having endured his own episodes of depression, King Solomon writes in Proverbs 18:14, "The human spirit can endure a sick body, but who can bear it if the spirit is crushed?"

If, as you read these words, you found yourself identifying with what has been said, it is absolutely essential that you exercise self-leadership and get the help you need to find relief from and remedy for your debilitating emotional state.

MASTERING OUR MOODS

Dr. Daniel Goleman, author of the runaway best-seller *Emotional Intelligence,* writes:

> A sense of self-mastery, of being able to withstand the emotional storms that the buffeting of fortune brings rather than being "passion's slave," has been praised as a virtue since the time of Plato. . . . When emotions are too muted they create dullness and distance; when out of control, too extreme and persistent, they become pathological, as in immobilizing depression, overwhelming anxiety, raging anger, manic agitation. Indeed, keeping our distressing emotions in check is the key to emotional well-being; extremes—emotions that wax too intensely or for too long—undermine our stability.[5]

If we are ever going to fulfill our Calling and achieve our life goals we will be required to learn how to master our emotions so that they do not end up mastering us. Whether we want to admit it or not, our internal emotions, in large measure, determine who we are and what we become. If you doubt this, consider the truth of Proverbs 23:7, where the wisdom writer pens, "As [a man] thinks within himself, so he is" (NASB). The absolute reality is that whatever is taking place on the inside of our life will ultimately work its way out into public view in the form of moods, behaviors, attitudes, and actions that will undoubtedly have an impact on our exercise of leadership.

That is why the apostle Paul, immediately on the heels of dispensing the counsel not to worry, which we looked at earlier from Philippians 4:6–7, continues by saying in verse 8 of the same chapter:

> And now, dear friends, let me say one more thing as I close this letter. Fix your thoughts on what is true and honorable and right.

Think about things that are pure and lovely and admirable. Think about things that are excellent and worthy of praise.

Philippians 4:8

Paul understood the connection between worrying and what we think about and focus on. There is a clear connection between what we think about and the way we process those thoughts, and our eventual emotional state. Our emotions are not formed in a vacuum. They are the direct result of how we respond to the circumstances and situations of life with which we are confronted—what Daniel Goleman calls the "buffeting of fortune."

One of the most helpful books I read as I began learning how to overcome and control my errant emotions is the work by David D. Burns, M.D., titled, *Feeling Good: The New Mood Therapy.*[6] In his book Dr. Burns espouses a clinically proven, drug-free treatment for overcoming depression. Though I have found the tools and techniques he offers extremely helpful in my own case, let me also hasten to add that I firmly believe that the depression some people experience is the result of biological and chemical factors that have been genetically inherited. It is difficult, and I believe dangerous, to dispute all the research that reports that some elements of depression and anxiety are genetic. With that said, let me also assert that even those plagued by depression and emotional problems that may be genetic in origin can still find a tremendous amount of relief by implementing some of the drug-free treatments presented by Dr. Burns.

Our moods, or the way we feel at any given time (i.e., anger, worry, fear, depression), are almost always the result of how we are interpreting and processing the events we experience on a daily basis. For some people more prone to depression and other uncontrolled emotions, such as anger, moods are often the result of a learned behavioral response to external events. For example, it is possible for two people to be exposed to exactly the same event but to be affected differently. Let me illustrate with a hypothetical situation: an unexpected financial reversal. Say two people own the same number of shares of stock in the same company. The stock plummets and both see their holdings reduced to nothing. For one person, the loss is processed as a challenge to be overcome and she redoubles her efforts to succeed and recover from the loss. At the same time, the other individual interprets the loss more personally and says things like, "I can never pick a good stock!" Or, "I deserve to lose my money; I've never been able to make money."

The way each of these stockholders responds to and processes the same event produces two different emotional states. For one person, the feelings generated may be those of renewed commitment and positive expectations for a better future, while the other individual may be overcome by feelings of failure and depression or anger as a result of the way he interprets the event. I have tried to illustrate this process graphically in the figure below.

When we are able to respond to events accurately and interpret them normally—no better or no worse than they actually are—then our emotions will tend to be normal.[7] However, con-

The Relationship between the World and the Way You Feel

It is not the actual events but your perceptions that result in changes in mood. When you are sad, your thoughts will represent a realistic interpretation of negative events. When you are depressed or anxious, your thoughts will always be illogical, distorted, unrealistic, or just plain wrong.

Thoughts: You interpret the events with a series of thoughts that continually flow through your mind. This is called your "internal dialogue."

World: A series of positive, neutral, and negative events.

Mood: Your feelings are created by your *thoughts* and not the actual *events*. All experiences must be processed through your brain and given a conscious meaning *before* you experience any emotional response.

194

versely, when we consistently interpret events through a subjective mental grid that tends to distort reality, our subjectivity will result in distorted emotions.

For people who regularly struggle with uneven emotions, such as uncontrolled anger, fear, or depression, it is almost always the result of this process by which events are distorted and irrationally or subjectively interpreted by the person experiencing them. The good news is that when this is the case, as it almost always is to at least some extent, steps can be taken to correct this unhealthy, learned behavior.

We Are What We Think

The apostle Paul's words are extremely sound when it comes to maintaining balanced emotions. Our emotional states, as we have already seen, will always reflect to some degree the focus of our thoughts. In Romans 12:1 Paul says that the key to personal and spiritual transformation is what we think about and those processes that take place in our mind. He says, "Don't copy the behavior and customs of this world, but let God transform you into a new person by changing the way you think" (v. 2). The way we think about things will have a profound impact on how we feel and the emotional states we experience.

In an effort to help us identify those negative patterns of thinking, which is the first step in overcoming them, David Burns lists ten of the most powerful patterns of negative thinking that produce negative emotions.[8] I will briefly explain some of the more predominant and destructive of these patterns.

ALL-OR-NOTHING THINKING

All-or-nothing thinking is extreme thinking that tends to see everything as black or white, one way or the other, but never a blend of the two. People caught in this negative pattern of thinking are constantly evaluating themselves and the events they experience in very stark either-or terms. "Because my church isn't growing, I am a terrible pastor, or worse yet, person." "Because my book proposal was rejected by a publisher, I am an awful writer." "Because I did not receive an adequate vote to be called as pastor of First Church, I must not be called to ministry by God." I think you get the idea behind all-or-nothing thinking. If this is a pattern that we have learned, it should not surprise us when we experience uneven or depressive emotional states—who wouldn't!

OVERGENERALIZATION

Overgeneralization is when we arbitrarily assume that because something has happened to us once, it will always happen to us. When I was twelve, I had my first painful experience with women. I was at Camp Silver Lake and asked a beautiful girl by the name of Debbie to our big end-of-camp banquet. Once I had finally worked up the courage to ask, she shot me down in what felt like a fiery blaze of rejection. As a result of that painful experience, I began to overgeneralize and assume that every girl I asked out would respond in the same way. It was a response pattern that caused me much unnecessary pain and anxiety throughout my teenage and college years. Because Debbie did not want to go with me to the camp banquet, I arbitrarily assumed that no one would ever want to go out with me.

MENTAL FILTERING

Mental filtering occurs when we isolate a negative detail in any experience or situation and choose to obsessively focus on it to the exclusion of other details that are more positive and balanced.

For example, when I began preaching, I focused on every little mistake I made and concluded that I was hopeless as a preacher and public communicator. Then when I had to begin preparing the next sermon, my focus still on the mistakes in the previous sermon, I was overcome with dread and fear assuming I would make the same—or worse—mistakes in the new sermon as well. For years this caused me great misery every Saturday as I began reviewing the next day's sermon.

196

DISQUALIFYING THE POSITIVE

Somewhat the opposite of mental filtering is disqualifying the positive. In this pattern we negate anything positive that is said to us as a form of encouragement or affirmation. This would frequently take place for me when, at the conclusion of a sermon during which I had made a mistake, someone would say, "Wonderful sermon, Pastor!" I would immediately respond on the inside by saying to myself, *See, it was so bad, they feel sorry for me and feel they have to say it was good.* That is disqualifying the positive, and it inevitably leads to negative emotions.

JUMPING TO CONCLUSIONS

If you have ever had the experience of walking into a room and seeing that someone is upset, only to assume that she must be upset with you, then you have experienced the negative thought pattern known as jumping to conclusions. It is generally very destructive and inaccurate when we make wild assumptions without any foundation. And yet there are many people struggling with depression and fear and worry all as a result of making assumptions about the words or behavior of others.

HELP FOR MASTERING MOODS

So what, if anything, can we do to be proactive in mastering our moods before they master us? Let me make a couple of suggestions that I have found helpful in dealing with my moods and emotions.

PHYSICAL ACTIVITY

Few things will foster feelings of depression, gloom, and despondency quite like living a life marked by physical inactivity, lethargy, and sloth. Our inner life and outer life are uniquely linked to one another. As we previously were reminded in Proverbs 27:3, what

197

happens on the inside of a person's life will inevitably be reflected on the outside—and the opposite can be true as well!

To quote Charles Spurgeon once again, "There can be little doubt that sedentary habits have a tendency to create despondency in some constitutions."[9] Thus disciplining ourselves to engage in regular physical activity is one of the best ways possible to combat depression and other menacing moods. The reality is that many physicians and psychiatrists are increasingly prescribing exercise as a normal component in the treatment of depression.

Not only will regular exercise and an adequate level of physical fitness help prevent depression, stress, fear, and worry, as well as other emotional maladies before they take root, but vigorous exercise can help reduce depression, stress, and the like after their onset. I cannot begin to count the times when I was beginning to feel the dark cloud of depression start to hover over my life, and a robust time of exercise completely prevented its full onset. Now that is not to say that during those times I was eager to exercise. Honestly, the last thing I wanted to do was exercise. But I have now learned that if I will fight through my feelings and engage in exercise, it will work its emotionally therapeutic wonders.

I strongly believe that all of the practices of physical self-leadership articulated in the previous chapter are absolutely essential to the mastery of our moods.

SERVING OTHERS

Another action that we can engage in that has the effect of mitigating our menacing moods is to consciously focus on serving others. By taking the time and emotional energy to focus on the needs and circumstances of others in an effort to effectively meet their needs through sacrificial service, I have often found relief from errant emotions and negative moods.

While focusing on the needs of others, I am forced to see how incredibly blessed I am and how much worse my circumstances could be. I am convinced that serving others is one of the ways that we give God's Spirit the space to minister to our own emotional struggles.

LEARNING TO THINK AND ACT RIGHTLY

Ultimately we need to understand as leaders that we are what we think and that our actions are the product of our thoughts. Thus we must learn to think rightly and biblically, which, in turn, will result in a balanced emotional life and stable behavior. Coming to the realization that how we have been processing and thinking about the events and situations in our life are largely responsible for how we are feeling and the emotions that we live with is the first step in mastering our moods.

As leaders it is absolutely essential that we learn to exercise self-leadership in the area of our emotions and moods. Even world-class athletes can be defeated by their moods . . . and so can we.

A SELF-LEADERSHIP WORKSHOP

1. Take some time to list your life values—from your personal constitution following chapter 5—that can be affected by your moods and emotions.

Values Affected by My Moods

-
-
-
-
-
-
-

2. List the moods you struggle with most frequently (anger, fear, worry, depression) in the order of their severity in the left-hand column of the grid below:

Mood	Negative thinking patterns that most contribute to your struggle with this mood	
1.	• All-or-nothing thinking • Overgeneralization • Mental filtering	• Disqualifying the positive • Jumping to conclusions
2.	• All-or-nothing thinking • Overgeneralization • Mental filtering	• Disqualifying the positive • Jumping to conclusions
3.	• All-or-nothing thinking • Overgeneralization • Mental filtering	• Disqualifying the positive • Jumping to conclusions

3. For each of the moods listed above, use the right-hand column of the grid to circle one or more of the negative thinking patterns that contribute to your struggle with each mood.

4. Now, use the information you have just recorded to see how your thinking fuels your menacing moods. In the grid at the top of page 201, list the mood in the far left column and circle the negative thought pattern that *most* significantly impacts that mood in the center column. Then, in the right-hand column, write exactly what you are thinking when controlled by that negative thought pattern.

5. Now, using a concordance or any other resource that might help, write out in the last grid on page 201 a new, more objective and biblically accurate thought pattern that better reflects reality.

Mood	Negative Thought Pattern	What I Think
	• All-or-nothing thinking • Overgeneralization • Mental filtering • Disqualifying the positive • Jumping to conclusions	
	• All-or-nothing thinking • Overgeneralization • Mental filtering • Disqualifying the positive • Jumping to conclusions	
	• All-or-nothing thinking • Overgeneralization • Mental filtering • Disqualifying the positive • Jumping to conclusions	

Mood	New Thought Pattern

9

INTELLECTUAL SELF-LEADERSHIP

PERSONAL LIFELONG LEARNING

The Rev. Dr. Roger Fredrikson is a personal friend who is for me a living model of a leader committed to lifelong intellectual self-leadership. Roger is an internationally known Christian leader and author who, at nearly eighty years of age, is still growing intellectually and challenging other leaders half his age to keep learning and developing their minds. Roger continues to preach and teach regularly across the country, and his teaching is fresh and always given in a context that takes into account the latest cultural, political, and theological trends and issues of the day. I have never heard him speak when I have not felt a renewed commitment to keep growing intellectually.

Fresh from a victorious battle with leukemia, Roger Fredrikson is fully engaged in writing yet another book. It is a book in which he works through and shares many of the issues God brought to mind during his battle with this disease—a battle that he says was as much an emotional and intellectual battle of faith and spiritual growth as it was a physical battle.

While many of his peers have settled for a life that consists of little more than a daily date with *Wheel of Fortune* and an endless listing of their physical ailments and struggles, Roger is living the life of an intellectual Caleb—still committed to exploring the intellectual hill country of life for the glory of God. His life serves as an example and sounds a clarion call to leaders of every age to keep growing and stretching their minds. He understands that when we stop growing intellectually, we start growing old, whatever our age may be.

THE BIBLE AND THE MIND

The Bible has much to say about the importance and primacy of intellectual development and growth. In fact there is an entire book devoted to the need for wisdom in daily life. Though much of the Book of Proverbs is devoted to the practical application of knowledge and wisdom to the everyday matters of life, it also strongly advocates the need to pursue wisdom in the broader sense.

The biblical understanding of wisdom involves not merely the acquisition of "head knowledge" but knowledge that contributes to our healthy and holistic development as people. Certainly there are few endeavors that require this kind of development more than effective leadership. It was for just such a reason that the wisdom writer penned his proverbs:

> The purpose of these proverbs is to teach people wisdom and discipline, and to help them understand wise sayings. Through these proverbs, people will receive instruction in discipline, good conduct, and doing what is right, just, and fair. These proverbs will make the simpleminded clever. They will give knowledge and purpose to young people.
>
> Let those who are wise listen to these proverbs and become even wiser. And let those who understand receive guidance by

exploring the depth of meaning in these proverbs, parables, wise sayings, and riddles.

Proverbs 1:2–6

Happy is the person who finds wisdom and gains understanding. For the profit of wisdom is better than silver, and her wages are better than gold. Wisdom is more precious than rubies; nothing you desire can compare with her. She offers you life in her right hand, and riches and honor in her left. She will guide you down delightful paths; all her ways are satisfying. Wisdom is a tree of life to those who embrace her; happy are those who hold her tightly.

Proverbs 3:13–18

King Solomon, generally accepted to be the author of most of Proverbs, also apparently practiced what he preached when it came to the pursuit of knowledge and intellectual development, as he wrote in Ecclesiastes 1:12–13:

I, the Teacher, was king of Israel, and I lived in Jerusalem. I devoted myself to search for understanding and to explore by wisdom everything being done in the world.

Our Lord also was an avid intellectual and pursuer of knowledge while he lived on earth. At a very early age he had engaged in adequate study and experienced sufficient intellectual development to challenge the teachers and priests of his day. We recall the episode where young Jesus was inadvertently left behind in Jerusalem because he was busy interacting with the teachers and priests. In fact Luke tells us, "All who heard him were amazed at his understanding and his answers" (Luke 2:47). Luke goes on to tell us that Jesus, God in human flesh, continued to develop not only physically but also socially and intellectually (Luke 2:52), establishing the pattern for all leaders who would follow.

The reality is that when it comes to the effective exercise of public leadership in today's pluralistic and syncretistic culture,

205

few tools are more essential than on-going, comprehensive intellectual self-leadership.

THE PRIMACY OF THE MIND

For the Christian leader, according to Puritan theologian John Ryland, "Next to the regulation of the appetites and passions, the most important branch of self-government is the command of our thoughts: which without a strict guard will be as apt to ramble, as the other to rebel."[1] In our increasingly pragmatic world of evangelical leadership, James E. Bradley, of Fuller Theological Seminary, writing on the much neglected topic of evangelical intellectualism and study, begins with the following statement: "While the characteristic activism of evangelicalism is one of our leading strengths, the emphasis on experience, spirituality, and ministry can lead us to minimize and, in extreme cases, even denigrate the importance of study." Bradley goes on to state, "Evangelicals are typically impatient with scholarship and disciplined study, and this has led to our being justly charged with obscurantism, extending, in some cases, even to an arrogant anti-intellectualism."[2] Though Dr. Bradley may be guilty of a small degree of literary hyperbole in an effort to make his point, one of the areas where today's leaders are faced with a significant challenge is in the area of maintaining meaningful, lifelong intellectual growth and development.

Evangelical scholar and theologian Mark Noll makes a similarly striking and persuasive case in his contemporary classic work *The Scandal of the Evangelical Mind.* He begins this penetrating look into the intellectual activity of evangelicalism by stating, "The scandal of the evangelical mind is that there is not much of an evangelical mind." He continues by saying, "Notwithstanding all their other virtues, however, American evangelicals are not exemplary for their thinking, and they have not been so for several generations."[3]

Unfortunately it would seem that an objective survey of evangelical intellectual influence on today's cultural milieu demonstrates that we Christian leaders have abandoned intellectual pursuits in favor of pragmatic practices that promise quick and tangible results.

I believe we have become guilty of accepting an intellectual frame of reference that is the product of an evangelical Christian subculture that often questions the value of intellectual pursuits and scholarship. In many Christian circles it seems that if an activity is not directly producing church growth and expanding the kingdom of God, it is abandoned in favor of activity that is more "productive."

Today's leaders are often more interested in the tangible and measurable results generated by focusing energy on pragmatic methodologies than in what is often considered the more esoteric pursuit of philosophy, theology, and thinking deeply about complex issues.

Many leaders today, particularly those of us who have come of age during the 1970s and 80s with evangelicalism's pervasive focus on the mega-church, are much more interested in "what works" than we are in "what's right or sound." This is not in any way to suggest that what's right and what works are mutually exclusive; however, the reality is that the two are not always the same.

DUMBING LEADERS DOWN

Unfortunately, reviving intellectual discipline among evangelical leaders has been made more difficult than ever before as the various genres of electronic media and entertainment have permeated the fabric of American culture.

Today we live in a culture where the sum total of most people's intellectual food, including that of all too many leaders, comes predigested in the form of televised sound bites and highly biased "news" reporting. It can be safely said that often television and its producers exercise substantially more influence over our life than we leaders do ourselves.

From television we subconsciously (and at times even consciously) absorb what it is we should wear and how we should look. Our political, social, and often even our moral positions are subtly and insidiously influenced, if not determined, by television.

This is not to suggest that there is some subversive conspiracy afoot to control the minds of people, but rather to say that a rapid and pervasive "dumbing down" has become a de facto reality in American culture.[4] Ability in critical thinking skills, logical analysis of important issues, and rational problem-solving skills is at an all-time low among high school and college students in our country.

During the final years of the twentieth century and the beginning of the twenty-first century, it has become a sad reality that the primary issues of public discourse and debate are more often than not predetermined and then framed by the media. This has become increasingly true as giant entertainment conglomerates have swallowed network news operations, causing them to further water down their coverage of complex issues in favor of more engaging, viewer-friendly, entertainment-oriented coverage. More and more we are encouraged not so much in *how* to think about important issues but rather *what* to think about these issues.

It has become too easy for leaders to simply adopt sound-bite positions they hear bantered about over the airwaves rather than to think deeply and critically about increasingly complex issues. Seldom do today's Christian leaders, regardless of the arena in which they lead, engage in rigorous study of primary sources in an effort to determine the most bibliocentric positions on the plethora of culturally relevant issues confronting them at every turn.

This has made for a somewhat paradoxical situation: While the cultural and societal issues are becoming increasingly complex with each passing year, our collective ability as evangelical leaders to think deeply and critically about these complex issues seems to be rapidly decreasing.

As leaders it is time for us to take seriously our need to exercise effective intellectual self-leadership so that we are able to skillfully guide those people and organizations God has entrusted to us through what promises to be an intellectually challenging future.

I wholly concur with Mark Noll when he writes:

the mind of the Christian is important because God is important. Who, after all, made the world of nature, and then made possible the development of sciences through which we find out more about nature? Who formed the universe of human interactions, and so provided the raw material of politics, economics, sociology, and history? Who created the human mind in such a way that it could grasp the realities of nature, of human interactions, of beauty, and so made possible the theories on such matters by philosophers and psychologists? . . . Who, moment by moment, maintains the connections between what is in our minds and what is in the world beyond our minds? The answer in every case is the same. God did it, and God does it.[5]

For these reasons we Christian leaders at the beginning of the new millennium must recommit ourselves to the lifelong discipline of ongoing intellectual exploration, growth, development, and inter-disciplinary discourse.

THE NEED FOR LIFELONG LEARNING

As I write this chapter I am sitting in a Florida hotel room watching CNN and reflecting on a dinner I just shared with a friend and mentor of mine, Leighton Ford. Leighton was one of the featured speakers at the denominational conference I am attending, which afforded us an opportunity to reconnect with each other.

Like Roger Fredrikson (also a personal friend of Leighton's), Leighton Ford is the kind of leader who is a lifelong learner. There has never been a time that we have been together or talked on the phone that he hasn't shared a few titles of books that are "must reads." Although he is in his late sixties and could easily rest on his more than abundant laurels, Leighton is constantly exploring new subjects and reading new authors. His mind seems to be constantly in motion. He thinks deeply about an assortment of diverse issues, and his spiritual life is in a state of perpetual progress. It is impossible to be with him for any period of time without being deeply stimulated at an intellectual level.

209

The result of this constant intellectual inquiry and processing is a noticeable freshness when he speaks and teaches. After Leighton spoke to our denominational conference, one of my colleagues said, "Leighton Ford seems to stay so fresh and relevant." It is a quality that everyone who spends any time with him immediately notices. At the same time, it must be said that because Leighton rarely accepts the predigested "party line" on complex issues, his positions can be very challenging for those more used to accepting whatever they hear or read in the media.

Several years ago Leighton took up painting for the intellectual stimulation and growth he said it provided him. Though he didn't have any experience, he took art lessons and now is quite an accomplished painter. A few years ago, as I was admiring one of his works in progress, he remarked that painting forced him to look at scenes in an entirely new and different way. Painting challenges his preconceptions and so he has continued to pursue this new challenge.

After every contact with Leighton I am stimulated and encouraged to keep my intellect sharp by being a lifelong learner. I long to have a similar kind of stimulating effect on the people I lead and meet. I want to have more than a shallow sound-bite position on the exceedingly complex issues with which we are faced at the beginning of the twenty-first century, and I know that can only happen if I am committed to continual intellectual growth. Yet the temptation is strong to lie back and rely on the information provided by the media for my personal perspectives.

PRACTICES OF INTELLECTUAL SELF-LEADERSHIP

As with each of the previous venues in which we must exercise effective self-leadership, there are several time-proven practices that can promote lifelong learning and ongoing intellectual development in the life of a leader. Though this is in no way offered as an exhaustive list, the following practices represent the baseline or minimum benchmark when it comes to intellectual self-leadership. These practices are study, reading, continuing education, and exposure to the arts.

210

STUDY

As Christian leaders it is vital that we engage in regular and rigorous study of not only theology and Scripture but also current cultural trends and issues that have a direct bearing on the church and people to which we give leadership. Today it is all too common for Christian leaders to hold theological positions and endorse interpretations of Scripture that they have come by secondhand as opposed to the result of in-depth personal study. In our current information age, the temptation is strong to simply adopt as our own a position that we have not thoroughly investigated. Then, with the best of intentions, we pass it on to others, who accept it from us, their spiritual leader, without question. They assume that we have come by it as the result of academic inquiry and honest personal study. But all too often, that is not the case.

Recently the denomination of which I am a part has been engaged in a significant debate regarding the extent of God's foreknowledge in the light of different theories concerning the content and nature of future reality. Though the commotion caused by such a debate has at times been draining, it has also led to a period of in-depth study for many of our pastors and leaders as they grapple with a subject of enormous significance.

When the debate was initially brought forward in our denomination as a subject of concern, the vast majority of our members had likely not given the subject much serious thought. Though everyone certainly had their opinion and position on the issue, not all of those positions and opinions were equally well-informed by the rigorous personal study of primary sources. More often, people were holding a position that they had accepted or inherited from somewhere or someone else.

Because the nature of the debate and subsequent vote had profound ramifications for our denomination, those called to cast a vote to determine the denomination's corporate position had to undertake much serious individual study. Though I am sure the issue is not settled with any finality, the debate was good for driving many of us back to the discipline of thorough study and intellectual discourse if for no other reason.

It is for this reason that I think it essential for leaders to be constantly engaged in the process of instructing others. Teaching others requires us to study in such a way that we personally own our positions and subject matter. Teaching requires that we be able to rationally support our positions when questioned and challenged by those we instruct. Being regularly involved in teaching others will force us to be engaged in fresh study.

The areas that we should study are as varied as they are numerous. Current events and cultural issues should be a part of our personal study regime. Theology and spirituality should be constantly explored as a way of expanding our intellectual growth. Specific subjects such as leadership, hermeneutics, church administration and growth, as well as other subjects of interest should be a part of our lifelong-learning repertoire. Nothing can substitute when we fail to regularly engage in intellectually challenging personal study.

Again, Dr. Bradley speaks poignantly to the issue of the spiritual leader's need to engage in regular study:

> Given the fact that the complexity of the human soul is at least as great as that of the body, what can possibly be gained by downplaying the importance of rigorous study of the Bible, doctrine, and Christian history? As Gregory the Great once observed, "Physicians of the soul treat deeper wounds than physicians of the body, and those who wish to be soul physicians without rigorous study are at least as dangerous as quack physicians."[6]

Ultimately the only way that we as leaders can provide fresh leadership that is free from the undue influence of the opinions of others is by keeping our intellect sharp through the practice of rigorous personal study. As leaders we are looked to for direction and guidance by those we lead. We must make sure that the guidance and direction we provide is the result of our own thinking and personal spade work, not merely the regurgitation of popular opinion. The people of God deserve no less.

READING

Another integral practice of intellectual self-leadership is the discipline of reading. Reading is essential not only for serious study but also for effective leadership.

At a conference I attended in Atlanta, Georgia, during the mid-1980s I heard Dr. Howard Hendricks deliver a spellbinding talk. One of the things he said during that talk, and something that has remained important to me to this day, is the statement, "Readers are leaders and leaders are readers." Today I am more convinced than ever that those words are absolutely true.

One of the things that has been most surprising and disturbing to me is how little many of those in positions of leadership read. I am not talking about the periodic reading of a popular novel, but regular, consistent reading on a wide variety of topics and genres in an effort to be as intellectually well-rounded as possible.

I have been shocked to learn that some pastors I have spoken with have not read a complete nonfiction book within the last year. As I have taught both doctoral level courses and undergraduate courses, I have been regularly disappointed to hear the moans and complaints of students when they initially peruse the reading list I provide. I have actually had students at the doctoral level tell me that they could not read a particular book—that it simply was beyond their intellectual ability to comprehend.

What is happening to our leaders when they resist reading and consider it an unnecessary burden? Unfortunately this response is becoming more and more common. It is a trend that we must reverse if we are serious about providing continued leadership that is effective and relevant in meeting the needs of an increasingly diverse culture that has evolved to the place where, as Francis Schaeffer has written, the majority of the population has an astonishingly limited "Christian Memory."[7]

What is it that we as leaders should be reading? What types of literature will provide us with the intellectual development we need to lead well in this day and age? I suggest at least five genres that should create the foundation of our reading: biography (memoir), current affairs, professional development, Christian classics, and contemporary Christian works.

Biography

Of all the genres of reading available, I am personally convinced that biography is one of the most instructive and beneficial for any leader, regardless of the type of leadership he exercises. There

213

is much to learn as we read the stories of those who have gone before us. The subjects of many biographies are people who have been influential in their particular field—in other words, people who have been leaders. From these leaders we can learn invaluable lessons that will enhance both our life and leadership. We will discover mistakes to avoid and disciplines to adopt. We can begin to see how God has worked in the lives of great leaders who have significantly influenced our culture and world. The benefit of biographies to the life of a leader cannot be overemphasized.

During the past year, some of the biographies I have read include: *Lindbergh* by A. Scott Berg; *Titan: The Life of John Rockefeller* by Ron Chernow; *Madeleine Albright* by Michael Dobbs; *Gore* by Bob Zelnick; *A Gift from the Sea* by Anne Morrow Lindbergh; *Sabbatical Journey*, an autobiographical account of the final year of Henri Nouwen's life; *Addicted to Danger* by attorney and mountaineer Jim Wickwire; and *A Pirate Looks at Fifty,* an autobiographical look at the life of musician Jimmy Buffet as he approached his fiftieth year.

I cannot express strongly enough the learning and insight that is available to a leader through the reading of biography. In fact I have never read a single biography from which I have not learned significantly and eventually incorporated into one of my books, sermons, or teaching curricula. Whether they are biographies of historical figures, political leaders, religious leaders and personalities, icons of pop culture, or adventurers, every one of them has been instructive in some way and increased my knowledge and intellectual development as a leader.

The reason I stress the importance of biography is because it is easy for all of us to limit ourselves to whatever our favorite genre is and neglect those that are less familiar to us. However, surprising and rewarding nuggets await us as we venture into unfamiliar literary territory and experience new forms of writing and literature. Every leader should make the reading of a biography a high priority.

Current Affairs

It is important to maintain our exposure to thoughtful analyses of current events and cultural trends by reading timely volumes from this genre.

214

In recent years, authors and leaders such as William Bennett have penned offerings such as *The Death of Outrage,* which is a must read for any spiritual leader in our present culture. *Roaring Lambs* by Bob Briner, *Business at the Speed of Thought* by Bill Gates, *Shadow* by Bob Woodward of Watergate fame, and *The Ethical Imperative* by Dalla Costa are all books giving a perspective of current events and culture that can be indispensable to the Christian leader intent on providing sound leadership during what can be for many a culturally confusing time.

Another extremely helpful tool that can provide an unending stream of reading material and intellectual stimulation on current events and trends as they impact the Christian leader is an audio magazine series called *The Mars Hill Tapes.* This is a monthly audio magazine that can be subscribed to that provides in-depth, intellectual analysis from a Christian perspective on many current trends. For information on this and other resources for intellectual development, see appendix C.

Professional Development

Another important area of reading for the leader is on topics related to professional development. It is vital to maintain constant exposure to the latest and best writing that deals with specific areas of our profession. Christian administrators and educators, directors of nonprofit organizations, pastors in local church settings, Christian executives, community leaders, and any other type of leader all must consistently be feeding their mind with new ideas for how to better and more effectively exercise leadership.

Though too numerous to mention by name, there are many books that deal with leading boards, preaching, church administration, the administration of nonprofit foundations and organizations, vision casting, marketing, and countless other helpful topics for leadership professionals.

Christian Classics and Contemporary Christian Offerings

Finally, our reading should be augmented by a balanced menu of Christian classics and contemporary Christian books. Authors such as Max Lucado, Eugene Peterson, Charles Swindoll, Henri

Nouwen, John Piper, R. C. Sproul, Michael Horton, Brennan Manning, and Dallas Willard, to mention only a few, should be regularly included in our reading.[8]

I have found it most helpful to maintain a balance in my reading. I will try to read a biography, followed by something dealing with current events, then move to a volume on contemporary Christian living, and so forth, in an effort to read as widely and effectively as possible.

Right now I am reading Brennan Manning's *The Ragamuffin Gospel* during part of my spiritual discipline time. In the evening I have been reading an adventure book titled *Seven Summits*. And while in bed I have been reading Bob Woodward's *Shadow*, a contemporary analysis of the modern presidency since Watergate. In this way I am exposed to three different genres at the same time.

CONTINUING EDUCATION

Another tool in our intellectual toolbox that we should regularly utilize is continuing education. It is vital that we expose ourselves to regular educational opportunities and the intellectual exchange of ideas and thought that accompany most such opportunities.

Whether this takes the form of pursuing an advanced professional degree or merely attending seminars for professional development, placing ourselves in a formal, structured learning environment is extremely helpful and important for stimulating ongoing intellectual development. In these contexts we may become aware of new authors we will want to read and challenging subjects we can explore. It is in relationship with other learners that our ideas and preconceptions will be challenged and our critical thinking skills sharpened and honed for greater effectiveness.

There is no substitute for a regular plan of continuing education. I recommend a minimum of two seminars every year and, more ideally, one such experience every quarter.

Failing to engage in formal continuing education will create ingrown thinking that can result in a parochial style of leadership, which will cause intellectual stagnation within the organization and among people to whom we give leadership. If we want to create an organizational environment where learning and intellectual growth are valued, we must provide a consistent example with our own life.

EXPOSURE TO THE ARTS

Several years ago I was introduced to a fellow fly-fishing enthusiast who also happened to be the resident conductor of the Omaha Symphony. Though I had always been an avid fan of music, my relationship with Ernest led me to a deeper exploration of the arts as an avenue for intellectual growth.

My wife and I became subscribers and regular attenders at the symphony's Master Works Series and began exploring classical music and art more vigorously. We began attending the lectures that Ernest presented before each concert, masterfully sharing with us insights into the composer of the evening and the various compositions that would be featured. We attended lectures at the Joselyn Art Museum where programs were presented exploring a certain genre of art and the music of that same period. It wasn't long before I began purchasing recordings of the music I had heard and even reading biographies of the composers' lives. One such program I attended on the French Impressionist period had a profound impact on me as I learned how the music and art of that time also reflected a change in theology that has remained with us to this day.

There is something about the arts (music, art, theater) that can deeply and profoundly affect us at an intellectual level if we take the time and effort necessary to enter into it with an open and curious mind. I am more convinced than ever that exposure to the arts on a regular basis is a vital, but often neglected, aspect of any leader's lifelong intellectual development.

TAKE TIME TO SHARPEN THE SAW

On numerous occasions when Billy Graham has been asked what, if anything, he would do differently if he had his life to live over, he has made the statement that he would have spent twice as much time preparing himself for leadership and preaching and half as much time actually leading and preaching.

Based on the fruit of this great evangelist's ministry over the years, the sentiments of that statement may seem somewhat misguided and unnecessary to many. And yet Billy Graham firmly believes that his ministry would possibly have been even more effective had he spent more time sharpening his intellectual and spiritual saw before he began actively cutting into American culture with his presentation of the gospel. I have become increasingly convinced over the last fifteen years that the Reverend Graham's words are laden with much wisdom that would benefit all leaders.

On Sunday morning, October 26, 1997, I awoke to a sight for which I was quite unprepared. As I opened our front door in Omaha, Nebraska, on that Sunday morning to let our dog, Ginger, out for her morning ritual, I was overwhelmed by a sea of white. During the night the city had been completely covered by an early, freak snowstorm that dropped eighteen inches of wet, heavy snow. Because most of our trees had not fully been disrobed of their fall foliage, the heavy snow was too much for most of them. The five large maple trees in our backyard were destroyed by the weight of the snow and had crashed to the ground, creating a jungle of huge limbs.

With the rest of Omaha, I was forced to begin sawing and chopping the fallen trees in an effort to clear my backyard. Not being lucky enough to own a chain saw, I began the arduous task with an old Skil saw I hadn't used in years. Unfortunately the blade on my saw had seen better days. However, because it was all I had, I attempted to cut my trees with this truly inadequate tool. While my neighbors were blazing away with their powerful, hungry chain saws, I labored fruitlessly with my dull, rusted old saw—it was an exercise of extreme frustration and futility!

Finally, after three hours of absolute frustration, during which time I had succeeded in nothing more than making a mess and sweating myself into a fit of cold-induced asthma, I decided it was time to get a new saw. With my new chain saw I was able to clear the yard quickly and, in contrast to my first three hours of hapless agony, effortlessly.

As leaders, we need to realize that time taken in sharpening our intellect and equipping our mind through the practices of intellectual self-leadership will not be wasted. In fact our leadership tasks will be easier and more effective in direct proportion to the amount of time we invest in sharpening our saw.

A SELF-LEADERSHIP WORKSHOP

1. On a scale of 1 to 10, how well are you presently exercising intellectual self-leadership?

Intellectual Pursuit	little or not at all			sporadic				very well		Score
Study	1	2	3	4	5	6	7	8	9	10	
Reading	1	2	3	4	5	6	7	8	9	10	
Continuing Education	1	2	3	4	5	6	7	8	9	10	
Exposure to the Arts	1	2	3	4	5	6	7	8	9	10	

Total Score:

2. To which aspect of intellectual self-leadership do you most need to give attention?

Study
Reading
Continuing education
Exposure to the arts

3. Take some time to consider two actions you can take during the next three months to improve the intellectual pursuit you singled out.

Intellectual pursuit I most need to improve:
Actions I will take:
1.
2.

Self-Leadership Action Plan

Throughout this book we have been analyzing areas of our lives that need self-leadership and making plans for how to best implement self-leadership skills into our routine. Following is a grid to help you summarize your plan for more effective self-leadership in each of the four venues we have discussed.

My Spiritual Goal:	
Elements/Practices	**My schedule of implementing plan** (daily, weekly, quarterly, etc.)
Example: Scripture Reading	Date: May 23, 2000 Beginning tomorrow, May 23, I will set aside 15–30 minutes for daily Scripture reading. I'll try mornings first, and if that doesn't work out, I'll try other times of the day (lunch hour, bedtime).
Scripture Reading	Date: _____
Prayer	Date: _____
Journaling	Date: _____
Personal Retreat	Date: _____

My Physical Goal:

Physical Resource Management

Elements/Practices	My schedule of implementing plan (daily, weekly, quarterly, etc.)
Example: Diet & Nutrition	Date: May 23, 2000 I will make it a habit to be sure I am consuming the best foods for my body. I will stay away from *overindulging* in Oreo cookies.
Diet & Nutrition	Date: _____
Weight Management	Date: _____
Physical Fitness	Date: _____
Personal Medical Care	Date: _____

Personal Rest and Recreation

Date: _____

Goal for My "Anger" Emotions:	
Negative thought patterns affecting my anger (whichever applies)	**Goal for each negative thought pattern affecting my anger**
Example: Disqualifying the Positive	Date: May 23, 2000 I will make an effort to think positively in all situations. I will look for the good in people and events in my life.
All-or-Nothing Thinking	Date: _____
Overgeneralization	Date: _____
Mental Filtering	Date: _____
Disqualifying the Positive	Date: _____
Jumping to Conclusions	Date: _____

Goal for my "Fear and Worry" Emotions:	
Negative thought patterns affecting my fear and worry (whichever applies)	**Goal for each negative thought pattern affecting my fear and worry**
Example: Jumping to Conclusions	Date: May 23, 2000 I will find out the details of a situation before jumping to conclusions. This will alleviate my fear of others talking about me behind my back.
All-or-Nothing Thinking	Date: _____
Overgeneralization	Date: _____
Mental Filtering	Date: _____
Disqualifying the Positive	Date: _____
Jumping to Conclusions	Date: _____

224

Goal for my "Depression" Emotions:	
Negative thought patterns affecting my depression (whichever applies)	**Goal for each negative thought pattern affecting my depression**
Example: Overgeneralization	Date: May 23, 2000 I will focus on what *can* be done versus what *cannot* be done instead of looking at the whole picture as too overwhelming, thus getting depressed about it.
All-or-Nothing Thinking	Date: _____
Overgeneralization	Date: _____
Mental Filtering	Date: _____
Disqualifying the Positive	Date: _____
Jumping to Conclusions	Date: _____

My Intellectual Goal:	
Elements/Practices (whichever applies)	**My schedule of implementing plan** (daily, weekly, quarterly, etc.)
Example: Continuing Education	Date: May 23, 2000 At least once a year I will take a seminar or class that will help me grow and be better prepared to be used by God.
Study	Date: _____
Reading	Date: _____
Continuing Education	Date: _____
Exposure to the Arts	Date: _____

226

CONCLUSION

As those involved in work of eternal significance, we as Christian leaders have been called to a life that demands the very best that we have to offer. In 1 Corinthians 9:24 the apostle Paul writes, "Remember that in a race everyone runs, but only one person gets the prize." He continues by saying, "Run in such a way that you will win."

In today's culture the leadership race in which we have been called to run has never been more challenging. At the same time we are witnessing an increasing number of leaders who stumble in the race and find themselves disqualified from finishing well. Sadly, many leaders in the leadership race make their way well into the second half of the race before they find themselves lying in a heap, scarred and bleeding along the side of the road as the result of a serious misstep that could have, and should have, been avoided.

Aware of this reality, Paul continued his exhortation to run the race well by saying:

> All athletes practice strict self-control. They do it to win a prize that will fade away, but we do it for an eternal prize. So I run straight to the goal with purpose in every step. I am not like a boxer who misses his punches. I discipline my body like an athlete, training it to do what it should. Otherwise, I fear that after preaching to others I myself might be disqualified.
>
> 1 Corinthians 9:25–27

That is what self-leadership is all about. Running the leadership race to win. Self-leadership is about learning to lead your life in such a way that you will finish well and not stumble.

Let us never forget for a moment, however, that the only reason we are in the race at all is because of the lavish, undeserved, grace of God that has been directed toward us in Christ. We did not qualify to run in this race on our own merits and we will not finish the race on our own merits alone—in fact we cannot. Self-leadership is not about working our way into God's good graces or persuading him to bless our efforts as a result of our self-discipline and serious-minded effort. It is about taking full advantage of this opportunity we have been granted to run for the eternal prize.

Self-leadership is about straining for the finish line until the final moment of the race. It is about running in such a way that we will not stumble to the side of the road or limp across the finish line in survival mode, but we will run to the end, acquitting ourselves well. Self-leadership is about leading our lives in such a way that we take hold of all that God has given us so that we might accomplish all those good things that he prepared for us to do before we were even born (see Eph. 2:10).

As the church of Jesus Christ continues hurtling through a new millennium of challenges and opportunities, it will be incumbent on the men and women God calls into the ranks of leadership to lead with an integrity and enthusiasm that is a true and accurate reflection of the One for whom they lead.

It is my prayer that *Leading from the Inside Out* will motivate and equip leaders to run the race to win, and thus obtain an imperishable crown that they can ultimately cast at the feet of Christ, the one who made it all possible, on that day when the finish line is finally crossed. To him be the glory forever and ever, ages without end!

PART 3

GROUP STUDY GUIDES AND APPENDICES

GROUP STUDY GUIDES

CHAPTER 1 WHY SELF-LEADERSHIP?

I. THE LOST ART OF SELF-LEADERSHIP

1. How do you feel about the concept that a leader's private life should in no way be relevant to his exercise of public leadership?

2. Why do you think the argument for a dichotomy between a leader's private behavior and her public leadership is so emotionally charged and polarizing today?

3. What might be some of the consequences of such a dichotomy if it were regularly practiced?

4. In what ways could a leader's private life bleed into his public life as a leader and impact leadership? Can you list some examples you are aware of?

5. How do you think this "private/public" concept regarding leaders has changed (if at all) during the past fifty years? Again, can you provide some concrete examples?

6. What do you think may be the source or root cause of the present incongruity we seem to be seeing between a leader's public and private life?

7. Generally, what has been the result in society at large?

II. WHAT IS SELF-LEADERSHIP?

1. In your own words, explain what you think the term *self-leadership* means.
2. What is the difference between management and leadership, and how does it relate to self-leadership?
3. What makes self-leadership, as defined in chapter 1, difficult? Where do you experience the greatest struggle? Why?

III. A THEOLOGY OF SELF-LEADERSHIP

1. What can you learn from the following texts about the importance of self-leadership?

   • 1 Timothy 1:18–19; 3:2–5
   • 1 Timothy 4:6–16
   • 1 Samuel 2:22–36
   • 2 Samuel 11
   • Numbers 20:1–13

CHAPTER 2 ARTICULATING AND EMBRACING YOUR LIFE'S VALUES

I. CHARACTER COUNTS

1. How would you define "character" as it refers to an individual?
2. How does character impact personal behavior?
3. Should a distinction be made between one's public and private behavior as it relates to character? Why or why not?

II. THE LITMUS OF BEHAVIOR

1. In what ways does our behavior reveal our values?
2. Comment on the quotes by Kouzes and Posner on page 38.

III. MAKING THE CONNECTION

1. How have you derived your personal values? Where have they come from?
2. Are our personal values always laudable and positive? Why or why not? Explain how this occurs.
3. How do values, broadly defined, relate with what we might call moral absolutes?

IV. THE ROLE OF VALUES IN LEADERSHIP

1. How do values play a role in leadership?
2. What are the potential consequences when a leader's values are in conflict with the values of the organization to which she gives leadership? What is the cause of this dynamic?
3. How have we seen this principle demonstrated in the United States?

4. Why is it so tempting for leaders to fail to do the necessary work in identifying and articulating their personal values?

V. *Identifying and Articulating Your Values: The Process*

1. After reading the appropriate pages, define in your own words what is involved with each of the steps in this important process.

Step one.

Step two.

Step three.

2. Why is this an important process for leaders?

Chapter 3 Connecting with Your Life's Calling

I. What Is a Calling?

1. Define Calling (vocation).
2. Define calling (avocation).
3. How have we confused Calling and calling in our present culture?
4. Why is it so vital for us as leaders to connect with our Calling? What might be the result of failing to do so?

II. Transcendent Meaning While Making Tents

1. Why do people long for a sense of transcendent meaning?
2. How does our Calling relate to our calling? Why are both vitally important?

III. Following the Clues

1. Based on your reading, list and briefly explain the seven clues that can help us find our best calling.
2. Based on the life of Moses, what are some additional insights you may have garnered relating to Calling and calling?

CHAPTER 4 LAYING OUT YOUR LIFE'S GOALS

I. THE POWER OF GOALS

1. Why do you think goals have such a powerful influence on us as people?
2. What is the biggest challenge you face when setting goals? Why? Explain.

II. WHAT'S A LIFE GOAL?

1. Give your definition of a goal.
2. What is a life goal?
3. What makes a life goal different than what are called S.M.A.R.T. goals?
4. Is there a role for S.M.A.R.T. goals in our goal setting? What is it?
5. What do you think the danger is in S.M.A.R.T. goals if they are the only goals we set?
6. What are six guidelines that can assist us in setting life goals?
7. Can you list some biblical leaders who had goals that would qualify as life goals? List them and explain in what way they were life goals.

Chapter 5 Measuring Your Life's Motivation

I. Something More Than Knowledge

1. In what ways does knowledge provide power in the area of self-leadership?
2. In what ways can knowledge be a liability to the exercise of self-leadership? Give some examples.

II. The Missing Link

1. Define motivation as it pertains to self-leadership.
2. What are the four key motivating mechanisms in our life? Give a brief explanation of each.
3. Of these four, which seems to be the most powerful motivation in your life? Why?
4. Which is the least powerful? Why?

III. Measuring Motivation

1. Apply the Motivational Factor Grid to another biblical leader as it was applied to Moses.
2. What can you do to increase your level of motivation, if necessary?

IV. When Motivation Is Missing

1. Describe the two exercises that are useful for increasing motivation.
2. Which exercise is most appealing and would be most effective for you? Why?

Chapter 6 Spiritual Self-Leadership

I. Personal Soul Care

1. In your own words, what is personal soul care?
2. Why is personal soul care an important part of your spiritual life?

II. Spirituality in Leadership

1. Why do you feel spirituality is becoming a more common topic when discussing leadership?
2. Can you think of a time in your life when your lack of spirituality led to leadership failure?
3. When your soul is in the state of acedia (spiritual apathy, boredom, and absence of passion), how do you restore it?

III. Effective Soul Care

1. How can using different versions of the Bible in our Scripture reading help us experience the mind and heart of God?
2. What would be an ideal location for your time of Scripture reading? Why?
3. When do you enjoy prayer most? Why?
4. What could you do to make your time of prayer more meaningful?
5. If you keep a spiritual journal, how has it helped you in your personal soul care? If you haven't begun to keep a spiritual journal, what is holding you back? What could you do to overcome this hindrance?
6. List biblical leaders, besides Jesus, who took time for personal retreats.
7. What prevents you from taking a personal retreat? How can you overcome these obstacles?

What would be (is) your routine during a time of personal retreat?

8. What are some of the obstacles to effective soul care? How can you overcome these obstacles?

9. Why is it important for a leader to be concerned about spiritual self-leadership?

CHAPTER 7 PHYSICAL SELF-LEADERSHIP

I. PERSONAL RESOURCE MANAGEMENT

1. Why is it generally acceptable for Christian leaders to be overweight? Why are they seldom confronted about their condition?

2. In your opinion, why do Christians tend to neglect the Bible's teachings regarding the spiritual importance of the body and its vital role in the fulfillment of our Calling?

3. What are some of the reasons that churches often sanction poor eating habits in the name of fellowship, while they would never dream of doing the same with alcohol?

II. THE ELEMENTS OF PHYSICAL SELF-LEADERSHIP

1. List the four elements of physical resource management: Of these four, which is the most difficult for you? Why?

2. What inappropriate views of food do you have? What can you do to change them?

3. Do you agree that it is essential to maintain a proper weight if we are to glorify God with our body? How does caring for our physical body glorify God?

4. If you regularly engage in physical fitness activities, what are the reasons for your doing so and how do you remain consistent?

   If you fail to regularly engage in physical fitness, what are the primary obstacles that keep you from doing so?

5. How does having regular medical checkups relate to self-leadership?

III. PERSONAL REST AND RECREATION

1. What is the biggest challenge you face when it comes to engaging in meaningful rest and recreation?

IV. OBSTACLES TO EFFECTIVE PHYSICAL SELF-LEADERSHIP

1. What are the three main obstacles to effective physical self-leadership listed in chapter 7?
2. Which one of these obstacles is the biggest challenge for you personally? Why?
3. List three specific actions you could take to overcome these obstacles and get on the road to effective self-leadership.

Chapter 8 Emotional Self-Leadership

I. The Menace of Moods

1. What are some of the ways that moods can be a menace to our exercise of effective leadership?
2. Of the biblical examples listed, which is the one that you can most relate to? Why?

II. The Bible and Our Emotions

1. Of the emotions anger, fear, worry, and depression, which do you seem to struggle with the most?
2. In what ways does/do this/these emotions plague you? Why do you think you struggle in this particular way?
3. In what ways do you feel the media promotes fear and worry within our culture?
4. How should you as a Christian leader combat this cultural influence?
5. Why do you think depression is so difficult for spiritual leaders to admit and deal with?
6. What could be done to make it easier to deal with depression among the ranks of spiritual leaders?

III. Mastering Our Moods

1. Why is it vital for leaders to learn how to master their moods and then effectively do so?
2. What can be the result when a leader fails to master his moods?

IV. We Are What We Think

1. List the five destructive patterns of thinking that can contribute to depression and other adverse moods.
   Which of the five do you most regularly struggle with?

242

Chapter 9 Intellectual Self-Leadership

I. Dumbing Leaders Down

1. What do you feel has been the primary cause of the decline in intellectual vitality among Christian leaders?
2. From your perspective describe the "Scandal of the Evangelical Mind."
3. In your life, what is the greatest challenge to being a lifelong learner?

II. Practices of Intellectual Self-Leadership

1. List the four practices of intellectual self-leadership given in chapter 9.
2. Of these four practices, which comes most easily to you and which is the one you struggle with the most? Why do you think that is?
3. Do you agree with the statement "Readers are leaders and leaders are readers"? Why or why not?
4. What is your favorite genre of reading? Which genre do you struggle with the most?
5. What are some specific actions you can take to broaden your reading?
6. In what ways will a failure to maintain ongoing intellectual growth negatively impact your leadership?
7. Can you think of any ways in which intellectual self-leadership would be particularly relevant for Christian leaders in our culture?

APPENDIX A

RESOURCES
FOR LIVING OUT YOUR CALLING

Here are resources to help you find your gifts, talents, areas of interest, and the best avocation from which you can live out your true Calling.

TOOLS AND ORGANIZATIONS

Wagner/Houts Spiritual Gift Inventory
Fuller Institute of Church Growth
Center for Leadership Development & Evangelism
PO Box 41083, RPO South
Winfield, BC V4V 1Z7
Canada
800-804-0777

Creative Leadership Ministries
Randy Frazee
817-274-1315
This organization offers a helpful tool for determining a vision for your life.

Network Ministries International
25108 B Marguerite Parkway, Suite 217
Mission Viejo, CA 92692
800-588-8833
www.networkministries.com
This ministry offers assistance in finding the best avocation to live out your calling.

Role Preference Inventory
Masterplanning Group International
407-330-2028

BOOKS

Deborah Dash, Martha Finney, *Find Your Calling, Love Your Life*. New York: Simon & Schuster, 1998. Though not from a Christian perspective and in spite of some principles most Christians will disagree with, there are, nonetheless, some helpful, thought-stimulating ideas in this work.

Laurie Beth Jones, *The Path: Creating Your Mission Statement for Work and Life*. New York: Hyperion, 1996.

Jane A. G. Kise, David Stark, Sandra Krebs Hirsh, *LifeKeys: Who You Are, Why You're Here, What You Do Best*. Minneapolis: Bethany, 1996.

APPENDIX B

PHYSICAL SELF-LEADERSHIP RESOURCES

Here are some web sites where you can get valuable help and information on the area of physical self-leadership.

www.acefitness.org
The American Council on Exercise (ACE), a nonprofit organization that promotes physical activity.

www.walkersurvey.org
An opportunity to analyze your physical activity from the Lawrence Berkeley National Laboratory.

www.ncsa-lift.org
The National Strength and Conditioning Association.

www.strongwoman.com
Weight-training advice from Miriam Nelson, author of *Strong Women Stay Slim*.

www.drkoop.org
A variety of health information.

Appendix C

Intellectual Self-Leadership Resources

The Mars Hill Tape Series
For information and a free review tape, call 800-331-6407. An outstanding ministry in the mold of National Public Radio's *All Things Considered*. Discussion and interviews with contemporary intellectuals providing analysis from an evangelical Christian perspective.

A Lifetime Reading Plan
To develop a lifetime reading plan, consider the book *The New Lifetime Reading Plan* by Clifton Fadiman and John S. Major (San-Francisco: HarperCollins, 1999). This is a resource that will help any leader maintain a balanced literary diet from all genres of literature and direct the hungry reader to a broad variety of titles that have impacted Western culture.

The J. P. Moreland Tape Ministry
6332 Glendale Dr.
Yorba Linda, CA 92886
Intellectual resources from one of the country's top evangelical scholars. Moreland is a Christian intellectual who embodies the principles of chapter 9 of this book. His book *Love Your God with All Your Mind* (Colorado Springs: NavPress, 1997) is must reading

for all Christian leaders regardless of the environment in which they lead.

First Things
PO Box 3000, Dept. FT
Denville, NJ 07834-9848
800-783-4903
A journal providing an intellectual analysis for current events from a decidedly Christian perspective.

NOTES

INTRODUCTION

1. C. H. Spurgeon, *Lectures to My Students* (Grand Rapids: Zondervan, 1972), 7–8.

2. Albert Edward Day, *Discipline and Discovery* as quoted in Ruben P. Job and Norman Shawchuck, *A Guide to Prayer for Ministers and Other Servants* (Nashville: The Upper Room, 1983), 91.

CHAPTER 1 *WHY SELF-LEADERSHIP?*

1. Warren Bennis, *On Becoming a Leader* (1989; reprint, Reading, Mass.: Addison Wesley, 1994).

2. James MacGregor Burns, *Leadership* (New York: Harper Torchbooks, 1978).

CHAPTER 2 *ARTICULATING AND EMBRACING YOUR LIFE'S VALUES*

1. *Omaha World Herald,* 1998.

2. Thomas C. Reeves, *A Question of Character: A Life of John F. Kennedy* (Rocklin, Calif.: Prima Publishing, 1997), 245.

3. James M. Kouzes and Barry Z. Posner, *The Leadership Challenge* (San Francisco: Jossey-Bass, 1987), 301.

4. Samuel D. Rima, "Governing Values and Personal Constitution," January 20, 1994.

5. Aubrey Malphurs, *Values-Driven Leadership: Discovering and Developing Your Core Values for Ministry* (Grand Rapids: Baker, 1996), 110, emphasis mine.

CHAPTER 3 *CONNECTING WITH YOUR LIFE'S CALLING*

1. *San Bernardino Sun.*

2. Ben Patterson, *Serving God: The Grand Essentials of Work and Worship* (Downers Grove, Ill.: InterVarsity, 1994), 54.

3. Richard A. Muller, *Dictionary of Latin and Greek Theological Terms* (Grand Rapids: Baker, 1985), 329.

4. Abbott-Smith, *Manual Greek Lexicon of the New Testament* (Edinburgh: T. & T. Clark, 1981), 228.

CHAPTER 5 *MEASURING YOUR LIFE'S MOTIVATION*

1. Arthur Reber, *Dictionary of Psychology* (New York: Penguin Books, 1995), 472.

2. Quoted in R. C. Sproul, *Willing to Believe: The Controversy Over Free Will* (Grand Rapids: Baker, 1997), 155.

Chapter 6 *Spiritual Self-Leadership*

1. David Benner, *Care of Souls* (Grand Rapids: Baker, 1999), 33.

2. Job and Shawchuck, *A Guide to Prayer for Ministers and Other Servants,* 64.

3. Kenneth Boa, *Praying the Scriptures for Spiritual Growth* (Grand Rapids: Zondervan, 1997); *Praying the Scriptures for Intimate Worship* (Grand Rapids: Zondervan, 1997).

4. Norman Shawchuck and Ruben Job, *A Guide to Prayer for All God's People* (Nashville: The Upper Room, 1990), 8.

5. Gary L. McIntosh and Samuel D. Rima Sr., *Overcoming the Dark Side of Leadership* (Grand Rapids: Baker, 1997), 193–94.

6. The best place to begin your search for a retreat center is the local Catholic church or a local Christian college. For more help, visit The Leadership Formation Services web site at www.leadershipformation.com.

Chapter 7 *Physical Self-Leadership*

1. See Stephen R. Covey, A. Roger Merrill, and Rebecca R. Merrill, *First Things First* (New York: Simon and Schuster, 1994), 37.

2. Nancy Hellmich, "For Health, Doctors Tell Patients to Take a Hike," *USA Today,* 18 May 1999, sec. D, p. 6.

3. *Unger's Bible Dictionary* (Chicago: Moody Press, 1966), 409.

4. Wayne Muller, "Whatever Happened to Sunday?" *USA Weekend Magazine* (4 April 1999), 4–5. Also see Wayne Muller, *Sabbath: Remembering the Sacred Rhythm of Rest and Delight* (New York: Random House, 1999). This is a book that will provide much practical help in this area of learning to make personal rest and recreation an essential part of the leader's life.

Chapter 8 *Emotional Self-Leadership*

1. "North American Report," *Christianity Today* (October 25, 1999), 14.

2. Barry Glassner, *The Culture of Fear* (New York: Basic Books, 1999).

3. Spurgeon, *Lectures to My Students,* 160.

4. Hank Whittemore, "Ministers under Stress," *Parade* (14 April 1991), 4.

5. Daniel Goleman, *Emotional Intelligence* (New York: Bantam Books, 1995), 56.

6. David Burns, *Feeling Good: The New Mood Therapy* (New York: Avon, 1980).

7. Ibid., 30.

8. Ibid., 32–41.

9. Spurgeon, *Lectures to My Students,* 157.

Chapter 9 *Intellectual Self-Leadership*

1. Quoted in James E. Bradley, "The Discipline of Study and the Spirituality of Christian Leaders," *Theology, News and Notes* (October 1998), 6.

2. Ibid.

3. Mark A. Noll, *The Scandal of the Evangelical Mind* (Eerdmans: Grand Rapids, 1994), 3.

4. See C. John Sommerville, *How Television News Makes Us Dumb* (Downers Grove, Ill.: InterVarsity Press, 1999).

5. Noll, *Scandal of the Evangelical Mind,* 51.

6. Bradley, "The Discipline of Study," 7.

7. Francis A. Schaeffer, *The Church at the End of the Twentieth Century* (Westchester, Ill.: Crossway, 1994), 43.

8. Here is a brief list of classics I believe every leader should read: *The Knowledge of the Holy* by A. W. Tozer, *Knowing God* by J. I. Packer, *The Screwtape Letters* by C. S. Lewis, *The Imitation of Christ* by Thomas à Kempis, *Confessions* by St. Augustine, *Lectures to My Students* by Charles H. Spurgeon, *The Reformed Pastor* by Richard Baxter, and *Between Two Worlds* by John R. W. Stott.

SUGGESTED READING

Benner, David G. *Care of Souls: Revisioning Christian Nurture and Counsel.* Grand Rapids: Baker, 1998.

Costa, John Dalla. *The Ethical Imperative: Why Moral Leadership Is Good Business.* Reading, Mass.: Addison-Wesley, 1998.

Ford, David F. *The Shape of Living: Spiritual Directions for Everyday Life.* Grand Rapids: Baker, 1997.

Jinkins, Michael, and Deborah Bradshaw Jinkins. *The Character of Leadership: Political Realism and Public Virtue in Nonprofit Organizations.* San Francisco: Jossey-Bass Publishers, 1998.

McIntosh, Gary L., and Samuel D. Rima Sr. *Overcoming the Dark Side of Leadership: The Paradox of Personal Dysfunction.* Grand Rapids: Baker, 1997.

Moreland, J. P. *Love Your God with All Your Mind: The Role of Reason in the Life of the Soul.* Colorado Springs: NavPress, 1997.

Reeves, Thomas C. *A Question of Character: A Life of John F. Kennedy.* Rocklin, Calif.: Prima Publishing, 1997.

Roizen, Michael F., with Elizabeth Anne Stephenson. *RealAge: Are You as Young as You Can Be?* New York: HarperCollins, 1999.

LEADERSHIP FORMATION
services inc.

Sam Rima is senior pastor of Central Baptist Church in Sioux Falls, South Dakota, where he is also the founder and president of Leadership Formation Services, Inc., dedicated to the identification and formation of future leaders. Sam holds a BA in political science from Eastern Washington University and the master of divinity and doctor of ministry degrees from Biola University's Talbot School of Theology. He has served as an instructor with the Walk Thru the Bible Ministries and has taught at Talbot School of Theology, Grace University in Omaha, Nebraska, and North American Baptist Seminary. Currently Sam serves on the National Board of Directors of the Baptist General Conference.

For information on Dr. Rima's workshops and speaking, contact:

Leadership Formation Services, Inc.
3100 West Ralph Rogers Road
Sioux Falls, SD 57108

e-mail: drSam@LeadershipFormation.com

For more information, visit our web site at:
www.leadershipformation.com